S0-AKH-943

State Songs

Anthems and Their Origins

John Hladczuk and Sharon Schneider Hladczuk

The Scarecrow Press, Inc.
Lanham, Maryland, and London
2000

SCARECROW PRESS, INC.
Published in the United States of America
by Scarecrow Press, Inc.
4720 Boston Way, Lanham, Maryland 20706
http://www.scarecrowpress.com

4 Pleydell Gardens, Folkestone
Kent CT20 2DN, England

British Library Cataloguing in Publication Information Available

Library of Congress Cataloging-in-Publication Data
Hladczuk, John.
State songs : anthems and their origins / John Hladczuk and Sharon Schneider Hladczuk.
p. cm.
Includes bibliographical references and index.
ISBN 0-8108-3723-4 (alk. paper)
1. State songs—History and criticism. I. Hladczuk, Sharon. II. Title
ML3551.H58 2000
782.42'1599'0973—dc21

99-088806

∞™ The paper used in this publication meets the minimum requirements of American National Standard for Information-Sciences—Permanence of Paper for Printed Library Materials, ANSI/NISO Z39.48-1992.
Manufactured in the United States of America.

This work is dedicated to all of the composers and lyricists whose lives and activities have made this book possible.

Contents

Authors' Note

As part of our continuing attempt to update our sheet music and brief histories, we would appreciate it if our readers would send to us, by way of our publisher, any new or additional or updated sheet music or historical information that they may wish to share.

Acknowledgments

In retrospect, when we think of the years that it took to bring this project to completion, the countless telephone calls that were made in pursuit of the finished project, the boxes and boxes of correspondence that we have accumulated as a result of both our telephone calls and our correspondences, we can recall only one single instance when a given person—immediately and categorically—refused to cooperate with us.

Indeed, there are so many people who have helped us with this incredible project. Of the people who have been the most helpful, we first want to recognize A.J., Amy, Jason, and Adam.

We now turn to the following people and organizations, each of which has been partially responsible for allowing us to bring this entire project to completion. Some we have spoken to in passing, while others have been enduringly instrumental in directing us toward closure. We express our gratitude to these stalwarts.

Alabama

Alabama Department of Archives and History (Mr. David K. Brennan, Reference Services Administrator; Mr. Edwin C. Bridges, Director; Ms. Frazine K. Taylor, Reference Division Staff); Alabama Federation of Music Clubs (Mrs. James R. Cabler); Alabama Public Libraries; Alabama State Council on the Arts (Ms. Joey Brackner, Folklife Program Manager); Alabama State Library; Birmingham, Alabama, Public Library (Ms. Jane Keeton).

Alaska

Alaska Historical Library (Ms. Marilyn Kwock, Library Assistant); Alaska State Archives (Mr. Dean Dawson); Alaska State Libraries (Ms. Karen Crane; Ms. Sondra Stanway, Library Assistant); State of Alaska (Ms. Sherry Taber, Head, Public Services); University of Alaska Foundation (Ms. Barbara Gleanson; Mr. Scott Taylor, Acting Executive Director).

Arizona

Arizona Department of Library Archives and Public Records (Ms. Amie Moore); Arizona State Capitol Museum (Mr. Michael D. Carman; Ms. Charlie Horton; Ms. Mary Johnson); Arizona State Library; Arizona State Museum (Ms. Sandra Harris).

Arkansas

Arkansas History Commission (Mr. John L. Ferguson, State Historian); State of Arkansas (Ms. Ann Clements, Historian; Mr. W. J. "Bill" McCuen, Secretary of State; Ms. Sharon Priest, Secretary of State).

California

California State Archives (Mr. Joseph P. Samora, Archivist II); California State Library (Mr. Dick Nichols).

Colorado

Colorado Historical Society (Ms. Catherine Engel, Reference Librarian); Colorado State Library; Daughters of Colorado (Mrs. Edward E. Kidneigh Sr.; Ms. Elizabeth A. Scanlon).

Connecticut

Connecticut State Archives (Mr. Mark H. Jones, State Archivist); Connecticut State Library (Mr. Stephen Kwasnik, Senior Librarian; Ms. Julia Schwartz, Government Information Services).

Delaware

Delaware Bureau of Archives and Records Management (Mr. Roy H. Tryon, Chief); Delaware State Library (Mr. Steve Newton, Reference Librarian).

District of Columbia

Washington D.C. Public Library (Ms. Kathryn Ray, Assistant Chief, Washingtoniana).

Florida

Florida State Library (Ms. Cindy Wise).

Georgia

Georgia Department of Archives and History (Ms. Joanne Smalley, Public Services); Georgia State Archives; Georgia State Library (Ms. Martha Lappe).

Hawaii

Hawaii State Library (Mr. Robert C. Herr, Librarian); State of Hawaii (Richard F. Thompson, Department of Accounting and General Services; Mr. Richard F. Thompson, Librarian).

Idaho

Idaho Historical Society (Ms. Guilp Ford, Research Assistant); Idaho State Library.

Illinois

Illinois Arts Council (Ms. Loretta Rhoads; Dr. Engle V. Zagas, Director of the Folk and Ethnic Arts Program); Illinois State Archives (Mr. John Daly); Illinois State Historical Library (Mr. George Heerman; Ms. Linda Oelheim, Reference Librarian); Illinois State Library.

Indiana

Indiana State Library (Ms. Cynthia Faunce, Reference Librarian; Ms. Patty Matkovic, Reference Librarian).

Iowa

Iowa State Historical Department (Mr. Mark J. Barnes, Acting State Archivist); Iowa State Historical Society (Mr. Mark J. Barnes); Iowa State Library, State Historical Society of Iowa (Ms. Beth Brannen, Archivist; Mr. Gordon O. Hendrickson, State Archivist; Mr. Lowell R. Wilbur).

Kansas

Kansas State Historical Society (Ms. Jennie Chinn, Folk Arts Coordinator; Mr. Eugene D. Decker, State Archivist; Dr. Anne M. Marvin; Mr. Robert W. Richmond, Assistant Director); Kansas State Library; State of Kansas (Mr. Danton B. Rice, Legal Counsel, Office of the Secretary of State).

Kentucky

Kentucky Department for Libraries and Archives (Mr. James M. Pritchard, Archivist); Kentucky State Library; Louisville (Ky.) Public Library.

Louisiana

Louisiana Division of Archives (Mr. Richard H. Holloway, Archivist); Louisiana Office of

Cultural Development (Ms. Maida Bergeron, Louisiana Folklore Program); Louisiana State Library.

Maine

Maine House of Representatives (Mr. Edwin H. Pert, Clerk of the House); Maine State Library (Mr. Don Lamontagne); Maine State Museum (L. Cobb); Office of the Governor, Augusta, Maine (Ms. Norine C. Jewell, Legislative Counsel; Mr. John R. McKernan, Governor); State of Maine (Mr. Rodney S. Quinn, Secretary of State).

Maryland

Maryland State Archives (Ms. Susan R. Cummings, Archivist III); Maryland State Library (Ms. Shirley A. Rittenhouse, Librarian III).

Massachusetts

Commonwealth of Massachusetts (Ms. Lynn Frazer, Press Office Manager, Executive Department; Mr. Roy Lyons, Communications Office); Massachusetts Archives at Columbia Point (Mr. Richard C. Kaplan, Reference Archivist); Massachusetts State Library; Office of the Massachusetts Secretary of State (Mr. Steven P. Kfoury).

Michigan

Michigan State Archives (Mr. LeRoy Barnett, Archivist); Michigan State Library.

Minnesota

Minnesota Historical Society (Ms. Alissa Wiener, Reference Librarian); Minnesota State Library.

Mississippi

Mississippi State Library.

Missouri

Missouri Historical Review (Ms. Mary K. Dains, Associate Editor); Missouri State Library; State Historical Society of Missouri (Mrs. Elizabeth Bailey, Reference Specialist); State of Missouri (Mr. Roy D. Blunt, Secretary of State; Ms. Patricia M. Luebbert, Reference Supervisor, Office of Secretary of State; Mr. William L. Newcomb Jr., Chief Counsel, Office of the Secretary of State).

Montana

Montana Historical Society (Ms. Ellen H. Arguimbau, Reference Librarian); Montana State Library.

Nebraska

Nebraska State Historical Society (Ms. Sherrill F. Daniels; Ms. Betty Loudon, Research Associate; Mr. Dennis D. Madden, Audio-Visual Coordinator); Nebraska State Library.

Nevada

Nevada Historical Society (Mr. Phillip Earl); Nevada State Library and Archives (Ms. Leslie M. Hester, Reference Librarian and State Archivist; Mr. Jeffrey M. Kintop, Curator, Manuscripts and Archives; Mr. Frank C. Mevers, Director and State Archivist).

New Hampshire

New Hampshire Department of State; New Hampshire State Library (Ms. Zelda Moore, Reference Librarian).

New Jersey

New Jersey Division of Archives and Records Management (Mr. Karl J. Niederer, Chief of Archives); New Jersey State Library; New Jersey State Publications (Mr. Robert Lupp, Supervisor).

New Mexico

New Mexico State Library; State of New Mexico, State Records Center and Archives (Mr. Robert Torrez, State Historian; Mr. J. Richard Salazar, Chief of Archival Services); State of New Mexico (Ms. Rebecca Vigil-Giron, Secretary of State).

New York

Buffalo and Erie County Public Library; New York (City) Public Library; New York State Library (Ms. Christine M. Beauregard, Assistant Librarian).

North Carolina

North Carolina Department of Cultural Resources (Mr. Jerry L. Cross, Researcher; Mr. Jeffery J. Crow, Administrator, Historical Publications Section).

North Dakota

North Dakota Institute for Regional Studies (Mr. John Nye, Archivist); North Dakota State Library; State Historical Society of North Dakota (Mr. Forrest Daniel, Reference Specialist; Ms. Denise Haberstroh, Reference Specialist; Mr. George Newborg, State Archivist).

Ohio

Ohio Historical Society (Mr. Charles Arp; Ms. Arlene J. Peterson, Archivist); Ohio State Bar Association; Ohio State Library; Supreme Court of Ohio.

Oklahoma

Oklahoma Cattlemen's Association (Mr. Ellis Freeny, Executive Vice President); Oklahoma Department of Libraries (Ms. Betty J. Mathis, Oklahoma Research Librarian); Oklahoma State Library.

Oregon

Oregon Historical Society (Ms. Annette Bartholomae, Research Assistant); Oregon State Library (Ms. Layne Sawyer, Deputy Oregon State Archivist).

Pennsylvania

Free Library of Philadelphia; Pennsylvania Division of Archives and Manuscripts (Mr. Jonathan R. Strayer, Assistant Archivist); Pennsylvania Historical and Museum Commission (Mr. John B. B. Trussell, Chief, Division of History); Pennsylvania House of Representatives (Ms. Sandra L. Bennett, Executive Director, Government Committee; Representative Frank L. Oliver); State Library of Pennsylvania (Mr. Bill Nork, Reference Librarian).

Rhode Island

Providence, Rhode Island, Public Library; Rhode Island Historical Society (Mr. Michael J.

Costello); Rhode Island State Archives (Ms. Phyllis C. Silva); Rhode Island State Legislature (Senator John Celona); State of Rhode Island (Ms. Susan Bowan, Governor's Office; Mr. Henry Kinch, Office of Secretary of State; Mr. Jeff Taylor, Senate Majority Leader's Office).

South Carolina

McKissick Museum (Dr. Douglas DeNatale, South Carolina Folk Arts Coordinator); South Carolina State Library (Ms. Mary Bostick, Documents Librarian).

South Dakota

South Dakota Historical Society (Mr. John Borst; Ms. Marvene Riis, Manuscript Curator; Ms. Linda Somer, State Archivist); South Dakota State Library.

Tennessee

Chattanooga (Tenn.) Writers Club; Tennessee Historical Society (Ms. Ann Toplovich); Tennessee State Library and Archives (Ms. Mary Dessypris, Reference Librarian; Mr. Edwin S. Gleaves, State Librarian and Archivist).

Texas

Texas State Archives (Mr. Michael R. Green, Reference Archivist); Texas State Library (Ms. Cynthia J. Beeman, Research Assistant).

Utah

Utah State Archives (Ms. Terry B. Ellis, Research Center; Mr. Jeffery O. Johnson, Archivist); Utah State Historical Society (Ms. Linda Thatcher, Librarian); Utah State Library.

Vermont

Vermont Public Records Division (Mr. A. John Yacavoni, Assistant Director); Vermont State Archives (Mr. D. Gregory Sanford, State Archivist); Vermont State Library.

Virginia

Virginia State Library and Archives (Mrs. Jane R. Baugh, Head of Reference; Ms. Audrey Marrinan, Reference Librarian; Ms. Phyllis M. Young, Assistant Director of Public Services; Ms. Ella Gaines Yates, Librarian).

Washington

Office of Secretary of State (Ms. Pat Hopkins, Research Archivist); State of Washington Department of Trade and Economic Development (Ms. Bobbi Bennett, Information Services Program Manager); Washington State Library.

West Virginia

West Virginia Archives and History Department (Ms. Jamie Lynch); West Virginia State Library.

Wisconsin

State Historical Society of Wisconsin (Mr. Howard Kanetzke, Curator of Education); Wisconsin Legislative Reference Bureau (Mr. A. Peter Cannon, Research Analyst); Wisconsin State Library.

Wyoming

Wyoming Historical Society (J. H. Jameson); Wyoming State Archives (Ms. Ann Nelson, Archivist Research Analyst); Wyoming State Library.

Individuals

Ms. Adele Abrahamse; Mr. B. Drummond Ayres Jr.; Mr. John Bava; Mr. Franz Baydock; Ms. Iris Bell; Ms. Sylvia Bennett; Ms. Emily Benton; Ms. Monica Berger; Mr. Joey Brackner; Ms. Felice Bryant; Mr. Hoagy B. Carmichael; Ms. Kathryn Chester; Mr. Bill Coplay; Mr. Steve Cranford; Mr. Kenneth E. Crouch; Ms. Kathleen Daniels; Mr. Harry Dichter; Mr. Jim Dorsey; Ms. Melinda Feifert; Mr. Jim Fras; Ms. Lisa Gafton; Mr. Simon Galperin; Ms. Patty Gordon; Ms. Janette Gould; Ms. Julia Stacy Gould; Mr. B. E. Grantham Jr.; Ms. Elizabeth Gussen; Dr. Robert Haas; Mr. Charlie Hall; Mrs. Walter Hammerstrom; Mr. Orlin Hammitt; Mr. Don Hartman; Mr. Selford Hatcher; Mr. Thomas Hatcher; Ms. Susan Hayden; Ms. Bobbie Hayes; Mr. Clarence H. Hogue; Ms. Kerry Jones; Mr. Steve Karmen; Ms. Betty Kellogg; Mr. Edward A. Khoury; Mr. Gary Klaff; Mr. Bill Koch; Mr. Steve Larson; Mr. Amadeo Lucero Jr.; Mrs. Amadeo Lucero Jr.; Mrs. Francis C. McDonald; Mrs. McQuirter; Dr. Bobby Morrow; Mr. Joe Mosca; Mr. C. Haskell Newman; Ms. Amy O'Neill; Ms. Robin Perry; Mr. Bob Pinson; Ms. Suzanne Prokasy; Mr. Donald H. Putnam; Ms. Karen Quinn; Ms. Louredes Richter; Mr. Wallace Rodgers; Mr. Frank S. Rosario; Mr. Jack Rosner; Ms. Mary Russell; Ms. Mary Ryan; Mr. Paul Saylor; Mrs. Elizabeth Frances Scanlon; Ms. Jennifer Soper, Ms. Marvaline Stamphill; Mrs. Martha Talcott; Ms. Maureen Taylor; Ms. Mary C. Ternes; Mr. Ivan Trive; Mrs. Thelma King Tuiteleleapaga; Ms. Lynne Weber; Mr. Paul Well; Mr. Tom White; Ms. Mary Wyatt.

Periodicals

Atlanta Constitution; Atlanta Journal; Atlanta Weekly (Ms. Mary Ellen Pettigrew, Editor); *Iowa Official Register* (Mr. Tim Menke, Editor); *Knoxville News-Sentinel* (Ms. Idonna Tillery); *New York Times* (Ms. Vicki White, National News Desk); *Omaha World-Herald* (Mr. James Denny); *Oregonian; Sou'wester* (Mr. Larry Weathers, Editor); *State* (Mr. Jim Duff, Editor); *Syracuse Post-Standard* (Mr. Fred Fiske); *Texas Almanac* (Mr. Mike Kingston, Editor).

Other Governmental

The Territory of American Samoa (Mrs. Sopo Etimani, Records Management Specialist, Office of Archives and Records Management; Mr. Robert McDonnell, Territorial Archivist); Library of Congress, Copyright Office (Ms. Gillan G. Anderson, Music Specialist); Federated States of Micronesia (Ms. Sandy Heffelfinger); Office of the Governor, Commonwealth of the Northern Mariana Islands; Republic of Palau Register of Historic Places (Mr. David Orak, Registrar); Archivo General de Puerto Rico (Milagros Pepin Rivera); Smithsonian Archive Center (Mr. John Flexner); St. Thomas (Virgin Islands) Public Library; Virgin Islands, Department of Libraries (Ms. June A. V. Lindquist, Librarian).

Businesses

Bailey School Supply (Ms. Margo Bean); BMI; the Dreiser Trust (Mr. Harold J. Dies); Eastman & Eastman; Hal-Leonard Corporation (Ms. Jeni Elliott and Ms. Denise Dumke, Permissions

Administrators); the Jackson Board of Realtors; the Pioneer Museum; SESAC; Shodair Children's Hospital (Ms. Mary Lou Eggan, Financial Development Department Mr. Bud Iwen, Foundation Director); the Shoeford-Haffner Funeral Home; The Thomas-McAfee Funeral Home; TRO–The Richmond Organization (Ms. Judy Bell and Ms. Evelyn Sasko); Warner Bros. Publications U.S. Inc. (Mr. Dave C. Olsen, Director/Business Affairs).

Publishers

Dover Publications; Greenwood Press; Liveright Publishing; Edwin H. Morris & Company (Mr. David Bickman, Permissions Manager); Shawnee Press, Inc. (Mr. Steve Kanych, Administrator); University Press of Hawaii (Ms. Iris Wiley, Executive Editor; Ms. Jean Brady, Editor); University Press of Kentucky (Ms. Susan Hayden, Editor); Wisconsin Blue Book (Dr. H. Rupert Theobald, Chief Editor); WORD, Inc. (Ms. Lu Ann Inman, Copyright/Permissions).

Music Publishers and Organizations

ASCAP (Ms. Kathy O'Neill); Australian Performing Right Association Limited (Mr. John Dowling, Senior Officer); Capitol Music Company; Clark-Jones Music; Country Music Foundation Press (Mr. Paul Kingsbury, Editor); Country Music Hall of Fame and Museum (Mr. Ron Pugh, Director); Denny Music Group (Mr. John E. Denny, President; Mr. Jeff Taylor); Elsmere Music; Carl Fischer Music (Mr. Carl Michaelson, Manager); Galperin Music; International Ambassadors of Music (Mr. Merton Utgaard, Executive Director); Jack's House of Music; Maytan Music Center; the Music Mart (Mr. Wayne Snow); Opryland Music Group (Ms. Wanda Kilgore; Joanne Montella); Panhandle Music (Ms. Violet Forbes); Theodore Presser Company (Mr. Arnold Broido, President); Presser Music (Mrs. Martha Cox); Rice Music House; Schaum Publications (Mr. Wesley Schaum, President); Schmidt Music; The Smithsonian (Mr. John Hasse, Curator of American Music); Southern Music Company (Mr. Arthur J. Ephross, Director of Publications); Alan Taylor Music Company; Vester Music (Mr. James Vester); the Willis Music Co. (Mr. David B. Engle, Editor).

Colleges and Universities

The University of Alabama; Ms. Marilyn Thomas, Auburn University Library; Buffalo State College Library; Mr. Victor T. Cardell, Head, Archive of Popular American Music, University of California, Los Angeles; Ms. Darlene E. Fawver, Music Librarian, Converse College; The William Stanley Hoole Library; Mr. Gerald R. Reynolds, Acting Financial Vice President, University of Idaho; Georgia State University; Indiana University, Lilly Library; Ms. Sue Presnell, Librarian, Indiana University Library; Ms. Mary Russell, Archive of Traditional Music, Indiana University, Professor Tom Davis, University of Iowa; Ms. Peg Peterson, Department of Alumni Relations, University of Minnesota; State University of New York at Buffalo Library; University of North Dakota, Music Department; Mr. James Hill, Library, University of South Carolina; University of Virginia Library (Mr. Michael Plunkett, Curator of Manuscripts and Special Collections).

We have tried to make our acknowledgments comprehensive. We believe, however, that there might be persons out there whom we have omitted. To those people we do want to express our apologies and, again, our heartfelt thanks for helping us with this project.

Introduction

Overview

It has taken us the better part of ten years to complete this book. First and foremost, this book has been a labor of love and discipline and patience. It is not unlike a child—sometimes cute, sometimes funny, sometimes problematic, but always yours.

This book has come to represent many different things to us in many different ways. It has been at once secretarial, archival, historical, musical, sociological, psychological, emotional, and proprietary. We have spent so much time being so close to the songs and the histories of those who have created them that they are, in some very real ways, like family.

The idea seemed fairly simple when we started: there are fifty states, each has a state song, the state historical society should know exactly the who, what, where, when, how, and why of the song—so simple, indeed, that it truly amazed us that no one else had thought about doing a book that would end up being so easy. This was a quintessential case of "famous last words."

Though this ended up being a far more complex undertaking than we anticipated, through our research, we discovered a part of our collective history. Songs whose charms became evident in playing them suddenly became wondrously three-dimensional as we learned the histories of the people and the times surrounding each one of them.

What we have compiled here are the official state song(s) of each state. It is important that the reader know that there are official state songs and there are unofficial state songs. Also, there are state marches, state waltzes, state rock songs, state hymns, and on and on. But it is also important to bear in mind that each state song is unique in its circumstances. It might seem that these songs in sharing the designation of "official state song" might somehow be similar, yet there is only that designation to tie them together.

This book has a commitment to historical accuracy. Wherever and whenever possible, we have attempted to include the earliest extant copy of the sheet music for a given song. Indeed, some of the songs we could only find in hand-scored versions—no commercially printed versions exist. Also, we doubt that there is even a double-digit percentage of people out there who have ever seen an original Stephen Foster score, yet so much of his music has helped to shape this country, including songs like "Beautiful Dreamer," "Old Folks at Home," "My Old Kentucky Home," "Camptown Races," "Jeannie with the Light Brown Hair," and "Oh! Susanna."

The end result of all this is that we believe that we have not only captured a part of musical Americana but also have had a splendid—and rare—opportunity to view the parts that make up the sum of who we, as Americans, are today.

Methodology

The methodology to the collecting of our materials was, in retrospect, an exercise in natural evolution and expansion devolving from our initial idea for this book. Put differently, what began so simply became increasingly more involved with each step along the way. It was not, however, until we were knee deep into the swamp that we realized that "being easy" was the exception rather than the rule.

Initially, this book was intended simply as a compilation of the sheet music, nothing else. We began, quite assuredly, by going to an *Information*

Please Almanac and a current encyclopedia and simply recording what was listed as the state song for each state. Next, we wrote a letter of introduction to the appropriate state historical society, informing them of what we were doing and that we were looking to acquire a copy of the sheet music. We were amazed by what we got in return.

We discovered that although most of the state historical societies could give us the basic information about the state's song, few were able to supply us with sheet music. And much of the sheet music that we did receive was of such poor quality that we knew immediately that it would not be reproducible for publication. We also found that the state historical societies knew more about the history of the song than they knew where to find a good clean copy of the sheet music or where to locate the owner(s) of the song(s). (Please note that the sheet music included is a reproduction of the original music. In the interests of historic preservation, the music was not reset).

Our approach to our collection of the brief histories paralleled that to securing the sheet music. We tried to find primary-source, brief histories—that is, those written by the composers and/or lyricists themselves. After that, we moved on to family members, historical societies, journals, newspapers, and so on. Often, pertinent information was scattered throughout the historical material that we received. In those cases, we wrote the brief histories ourselves.

Once we had the format of what we wanted—the earliest extant sheet music that we could find, the most primary-source brief history, and permissions (if necessary), the book became a relatively task-oriented effort. It was at this point that we became detectives and "professional telephonists." Telephone calls led to leads, leads led to telephone calls, and finally after ten years of work we were able to close the project.

In the end, looking back, we are able to reflect back on a process that yielded far more rewardingly pleasant surprises than disappointments. In fact, our only disappointments and regrets are that not all of our song owners—three out of sixty-two—gave us permission to have their songs included in the book.

For those songs for which we were not given permission or for which copyright could not be obtained, we suggest that you consult www.50states.com/songs for further information.

In conclusion, we evolved with our methodology in response to our environment. What could be more natural?

Conclusion

This book is an attempt to capture the historical imaginings of what it means to be an American. It is a commitment to—and glorification of—our past, as well as an investment in our future. Yet even now, state legislatures have been either "dumping" or attempting to dump the old state songs—or portions thereof—for "things" that might seem a bit more in vogue (read, oftentimes, politically correct). This book is not only timely, it is also a historical necessity—one that will help preserve America, that will fix our thoughts while we still have some historical thoughts to fix. In short, there is a point that stretches far beyond yesterday or last week—and we are not talking about last month. We, as Americans, are the product of what we have been through, and that we should not forget.

Alabama

"Alabama"

Alabama, Alabama, We will aye be true to thee,
From thy Southern shore where groweth, By the sea thine orange tree,
To thy Northern vale where floweth, Deep and blue thy Tennessee,
Alabama, Alabama, We will aye be true to thee.

Broad the Stream whose name thou bearest; Grand thy Bigbee rolls along;
Fair thy Coosa—Tallapoosa; Bold thy Warrior, dark and strong,
Goodlier that the land that Moses Climbed lone Nebo's Mount to see,
Alabama, Alabama, We will aye be true to thee!

From thy prairies broad and fertile, Where thy snow-white cotton shines,
To the hills where coal and iron Hide in thy exhaustless mines,
Strong-armed miners—sturdy farmers; Loyal hearts whate'er we be,
Alabama, Alabama, We will aye be true to thee!

From thy quarries where the marble White as that of Paros gleams
Waiting till thy sculptor's chisel, Wake to life thy poet's dreams;
For not only wealth of nature, Wealth of mind hast thou to free,
Alabama, Alabama, We will aye be true to thee!

Where the perfumed south-wind whispers. Thy magnolia groves among,
Softer than a mother's kisses, Sweeter than a mother's song;
Where the golden jasmine trailing Woos the treasure-laden bee,
Alabama, Alabama, We will aye be true to thee!

Brave and pure thy men and women, Better this than corn and wine,
Make us worthy, God in Heaven, Of this goodly land of Thine;
Hearts as open as our doorways, Liberal hands and spirits free,
Alabama, Alabama, We will aye be true to thee!

Little, little, can I give thee, Alabama, mother mine;
But that little—hand, brain, spirit, All I have and am are thine,
Take, O take the gift and giver, Take and serve thyself with me,
Alabama, Alabama, I will aye be true to thee!

The Alabama Federation of Music Clubs conducted a contest in 1917 for an appropriate original musical setting for Julia Tutwiler's poem "Alabama." Mrs. Edna Gockel-Gussen's composition won this contest. Through the efforts of the Alabama Federation of Music Clubs the words and the tune were adopted as the State Song of Alabama by an Act of the Legislature March 3, 1931.

Julia Strudwick Tutwiler was born August 15, 1841, in Tuscaloosa, Alabama. Her parents were Julia Ashe and Henry Tutwiler. Henry Tutwiler had received one of the first Master of Arts degrees awarded by the University of Virginia and was a progressive educator.

When Julia was about six years old, Henry Tutwiler established the Greene Springs School, called by some "the Rugby of the South" and other critics said that in some respects it was superior to the English Rugby. Julia and her ten brothers and sisters had their upbringing in the midst of this school. Julia and her sisters and daughters of neighboring families attended classes with boys, had the same assignments, and recited along with them. This school experience was an important influence later on in encouraging Julia to work for coeducation. Also, the religious convictions of her father had a deep, enduring effect on Julia.

Because of Henry Tutwiler's excellent judgement, very successful educational enterprise, and wise investments, Julia was able to attend a boarding school in Philadelphia. This was at a time when Southerners were very much opposed to sending a young woman to a northern place of learning where she might become infected with radical ideas. The outbreak of the Civil War in April of 1861 made it necessary for Julia to return home.

The Greene Springs School remained open during the War and suffered no serious physical damage; therefore, Julia's father was able to finance her travel and study following the War. She returned with her older sister to school in Philadelphia in the summer of 1865, and that winter she entered the newly opened Vassar College. In the autumn of 1866 she became a faculty member at the Greensboro Female Academy in Hale County, Alabama, and when the principal resigned in the summer of 1867, the trustees elected Julia as his successor. This was a liberal step in the Deep South of this period and is evidence of her ability and personality. She resigned this principalship in the summer of 1869 and became a teaching assistant at the Greene Springs School. She later studied languages privately in Virginia for a year.

In the summer of 1873 as she neared her 32nd birthday, Julia went on a tour of Europe. She left her tour to study at a German teacher-training institute run by an order of Protestant sisters of charity. Upon completion of one year of study there, Julia remained in Europe for the next two years.

From available evidence, these two years were a period of hard work and privation rather than a time of relaxation and pleasure. As a means of adding to her income and as a way of giving expression to her new experiences and ideas, Julia wrote pieces for American newspapers and magazines.

In the fall of 1873, when Julia was particularly lonesome for home, she authored the poem "Alabama." The first and unauthorized version appeared in the Tuscaloosa *Times* on January 27, 1875. By the time Julia returned home from Germany in 1876, she found her poem widely reprinted. This encouraged her to perfect it in diction and rhyme. Finally, an edited and approved version was published on April 24, 1881, in the *Montgomery Advertiser*. Julia's own preference was that her poem be sung to the tune of the Austrian National Anthem, but this particular air never caught on. Later, one of her associates suggested the old tune of "Harwell" because of its familiarity, and this was widely used until 1931, when the Alabama legislature adopted a new musical arrangement.

Through personal experience, Julia Tutwiler knew the sacrifices and hardships required if a woman were to gain an education and prepare for a profession. By tradition, teaching in formal institutions had been a male prerogative, and nowhere had this been more true than in the antebellum South. Although Julia Tutwiler turned to the private academy as a residue of southern educational tradition, she increasingly became aware of the importance of publicly supported educational institutions. It took faith and perseverance to advocate expansion of public education in the South in the late 1800s.

When Julia returned to Alabama in late spring of 1876 she accepted an appointment as teacher of modern language and English literature at Tuscaloosa Female College, a Methodist institution. This school had a reputation as one of the leading seminaries for women in Alabama. The level of instruction was from preparatory through "regular collegiate" curriculum to the graduate department.

Julia was selected to represent the *National Journal of Education*, a Boston professional publication, at the Paris Exposition in 1878. In 1880, she prepared a paper on women's vocational training that was read at the Alabama Education Association meeting that year. Her address was read by a man, because it was deemed "unseemly" for a woman to stand before a large number of men and talk. She said that although the favored role for a woman was that of wife and mother, still many women would have to earn all or part of their living. She believed that society as well as the individual was the loser when women were limited to unskilled and poorly paid jobs for lack of training.

In 1881 Miss Tutwiler was appointed co-principal of Livingston Female Academy. At this time, Julia Tutwiler was an energetic, warm-hearted 40-year-old woman of medium height and build. She had a friendly manner and assured bearing. Her hair was dark brown and somewhat curly. Her blue eyes were reported to be keen and alert. Her contemporaries were particularly struck by her soft and well-modulated voice. She gave little attention to matters of clothes and style. She was an unconventional classroom teacher, disliking pedantic lectures, rote recitation, and textbook memorization.

Subjects of special interest to her were foreign languages, biblical studies, and English literature. Miss Tutwiler often dramatized selections by providing a musical arrangement, by making use of oral readings and of speech chorus. Two teaching methods she used were visual aids and field trips. Field trips were especially unusual for that period. She also encouraged creative writing.

Miss Tutwiler ardently advocated state financial support for training public school teachers. She energetically endeavored to improve the curriculum, raise the entrance standards, and urged adoption of statewide teacher certification requirements.

In 1890 Julia Tutwiler was made president and sole principal of the Livingston Normal College, a post she filled until her retirement in 1910. By 1899, the college's course of study met the entrance standards of the University of Alabama. In 1907, the University of Alabama awarded Julia Tutwiler an honorary doctorate of law degree in recognition of her work in furthering education in Alabama.

Because of the extent and significance of Julia Tutwiler's activities both in Alabama and in the nation, she was included in a volume of biographical sketches of 1,470 eminent American women published in 1893. She was then 52 years old.

As a determined fighter against ignorance, inhumanity, and evil, she was acclaimed as "the purest figure in Alabama history."

As a result of her efforts, the state legislature in 1893 provided for establishment of a girls' school in industrial and scientific fields located in Montevallo. Also, in 1893 another of her efforts was rewarded—the first women students entered the University of Alabama. In 1898, she was successful in having a women's residence established on the university's campus.

Although busy as a teacher and administrator, Julia Tutwiler also found time to be an active reformer. It is to her credit that in December 1880 the Alabama legislature adopted a bill that required the county jails to be supplied with wholesome water, toilet facilities, and heat in cold weather. And in at least two other fields of endeavor, she also gave notable service—prohibition and abolition of war.

She stated in 1906 that she was "a member of quite a number of Associations which are working for the 'coming of the Kingdom': the International Peace Association, the Charities and Corrections Conference, the Prison Reform Association, WCTU, YWCA, Salvation Army, antisaloon League, *all* the different churches of this little town of Livingston." Miss Tutwiler also had many private benevolences, and the record of these, when added to her public humanitarian and reform activities, underlines Julia Tutwiler's devotion to the welfare of mankind.

Even though she suffered intermittent spells of illness after her retirement, her good humor didn't fail. The Alabama Department of Archives had requested a picture. In sending it, she wrote that her likeness might encourage young people to realize that homeliness need not prevent them from leading useful and happy lives.

After a lingering illness, Julia Tutwiler died of cancer in Birmingham, Alabama, on March 24, 1916, at the age of 74.

In 1933, a marble bust of Miss Tutwiler and a memorial tablet were placed in the rotunda of the Alabama State Capitol. Part of the inscription reads, "Julia Strudwick Tutwiler, teacher, poet, prison reformer, patriot, lover of humanity, beauty, and truth. Pioneer for industrial and University education for women in Alabama."

In 1953, Julia Tutwiler was selected as one of the first eleven persons named to the Alabama Hall of Fame.

When Edna Gockel was a little girl in Covington, Kentucky, her parents first became aware of her musical gifts when they heard her playing the tunes she had heard in Sunday school. Edna was first called on to play in public when she was a member of the "infant class" in Sunday school. The regular organist was ill, and a substitute had to be found quickly. So Edna Gockel was placed on the organ bench with her little legs dangling far above the pedals.

After several years of studying piano with a teacher in Covington, she was sent to Benjamin Guckenberger at the Cincinnati College of Music. Edna was 11 years old at this time.

At the age of 15, she was invited by Mr. Guckenberger to be his assistant when he organized the Birmingham Conservatory of Music. So she moved to Birmingham with him and Mrs. Guckenberger in 1895. Soon afterwards the entire Gockel family moved to Birmingham. For 6 years, Edna remained in Birmingham teaching piano and harmony, accompanying, and being church organist.

Then Mrs. R. S. Munger offered her the opportunity to study where she pleased, with whom she pleased, for as long as she pleased. She chose to go to Berlin and study with Mr. Guckenberger's teacher, Xavier Scharwenka. Not only did she enjoy lessons with Scharwenka, but also ensemble classes with the celebrated cellist, Van Leer, and composition and orchestration with Phillip Scharwenka. The most delightful times were on Sunday afternoons at the Scharwenka home where people such as Grieg, Strauss, and Humperdinck visited.

At the end of two years, she received word that Mr. Guckenberger wished to turn over the Birmingham Conservatory to her. Edna decided the practical thing to do was accept the directorship of the Conservatory.

Her first season at home was very full and a very interesting one. She had appearances with two different orchestras—one with the Cincinnati, in Cincinnati, and the other with the Theodore Thomas Orchestra when it came to Birmingham. Besides her other duties, she became organist and choir director at St. Mary's Episcopal Church and at the Temple Emanuel.

About two years after returning to Birmingham, Edna Gockel married William Gussen, a Philadelphia musician who was both a pianist and a violinist and was a charter member of the Philadelphia Symphony Orchestra. After their marriage, he relieved her of the responsibility of directing the Conservatory so she could devote herself to the teaching she wished to do and to working at her own piano playing.

She became interested again in concert work and traveled extensively giving piano recitals in many cities of the United States and accompanying many of America's leading concert violinists and singers. She appeared as a soloist with the Cincinnati Symphony Orchestra, the Boston Festival Orchestra, Chicago Symphony Orchestra, and appeared three times as a soloist with the Birmingham Civic Symphony. Also, she appeared in duo piano recitals with her daughter, Elizabeth. (Elizabeth, for a while, was director of the Florence Branch of the Birmingham Conservatory in Florence, Alabama.)

Edna was active in the Birmingham Music Study Club, serving for many years as director of the club's Treble Clef Chorus. This music club was affiliated with the Alabama Federation of

Music Clubs and the National Federation of Music Clubs.

When the Alabama Federation of Music Clubs offered a prize of $25.00 for the best setting for Julia Tutwiler's poem "Alabama," Mrs. Gussen's composition, written in 1917, won the prize.

In 1920, following the death of her husband, she again became director of the Birmingham Conservatory of Music.

She was President of Alabama Music Teachers Association from 1922 to 1923.

In 1935, at the age of 57, she celebrated her 50th anniversary as a concert pianist by giving a recital sponsored by the music teachers of Birmingham.

She died April 26, 1937, at her home in Birmingham after an illness of several weeks.

The Birmingham Music Club established a permanent piano scholarship in her memory.

The Chamber Music Society of Birmingham dedicated its library to her, "The Edna Gockel-Gussen Memorial Library."

The Birmingham Conservatory of Music established a William and Edna Gussen piano scholarship.

History by Jennie Lee Perry Cabler of Florence, Alabama.

Alabama

Julia Strudwick Tutwiler
Edna Gockel-Gussen
Al- a - bam - a, Al - a - bam - a, We will aye be true to thee,
From thy South - ern shore where grow - eth By the sea thy o - range tree.
To thy North - ern vale where flow - eth Deep and blue thy Ten- nes- see;
Al- a- bam - a, Al - a - bam - a, We will aye be true to thee.

Alaska

"Alaska's Flag"

The words to the state song, *Alaska's Flag*, were written by Marie Drake, a longtime employee of the Alaska Department of Education, and first appeared as a poem in 1935. The poem was set to music composed by Elinor Dusenbury, whose husband was commander of Chilkoot Barracks at Haines from 1933 to 1936. The Territorial Legislature adopted *Alaska's Flag* as Alaska's official song in 1955.

Marie Drake, author of the words to *Alaska's Flag*, the state song, was born February 11, 1888. In 1907, she married James Drake in Van Wert, Ohio, where she was engaged in social work with the YWCA and the Red Cross. They came to Alaska when her husband was assigned to work with the Bureau of Public Roads. In 1917, Lester Henderson was appointed first commissioner of education, and he hired Marie Drake as his secretary. She remained with the Department of Education for 28 years, retiring July 1, 1945.

Marie Drake assumed the post of assistant commissioner of education in 1934. She edited and wrote most of the material for the department's *School Bulletin* that was circulated throughout the territorial school system. The poem that later provided the words for the official state song first appeared on the cover of the October 1935 *School Bulletin*. In recognition of her devotion to the young people of Alaska, Marie Drake received an honorary Doctor of Letters degree from the University of Alaska in 1958. She died March 5, 1963.

History source: *Alaska Blue Book* (Juneau: Alaska State Library, 1985).

Alaska's Flag

Words by
MARIE DRAKE

Music by
ELINOR DUSENBURY

Marcia moderato

PIANO

f *rall.* *a tempo* *mf*

Bb Eb

Eight stars of gold on a

Ab Eb Cm F7 Bb7

field of blue, A - LAS - KA'S FLAG, may it mean to you; The

Eb Ab Cm Bb Eb

blue of the sea, the eve - ning sky, The moun - tain lakes and the

F Bb Eb Ab

flow'rs near - by; The gold of the ear - ly sour - doughs dreams, The

Alaska's Flag - 2

Arizona

"Arizona March Song"

The "Arizona March Song" was selected as the official state anthem in 1919. The words were written by Margaret Rowe Clifford, the music by Maurice Blumenthal.

Mrs. Clifford was born in Montreal, Quebec. She moved to Arizona during the time of the Indian warfare, about 1880. She taught school in Mammoth, Arizona, after which she moved to Cochise County. Mrs. Clifford was residing in Douglas, Arizona, when she wrote the "Arizona March Song." She passed on in Prescott at the age of 84 on January 19, 1926.

Mr. Blumenthal was practicing law in Douglas at the time the song was written. Later he moved to Phoenix.

"Arizona"

The words and music to "Arizona" were written by Rex Allen Jr. "Arizona" was adopted as an alternative state anthem by House Bill 2300 of 1982.

History compiled by Hladczuk and Hladczuk.

ARIZONA

MARCH SONG

Words by
MARGARET ROWE CLIFFORD

Music by
MAURICE BLUMENTHAL
Piano arr. by Ray Stuart

songs that will now be sung. Where the gold - en sun is
pres - ence of our God! While all a - round, a -
land is con - se - crate! O come and live be -
mf
flam - ing In - to warm, white, shin - ing day, And the
bout us The brave, un - con - quered band, As
side us How - ev - er far ye roam Come
sons of men are blaz - ing Their price - less right of way.
guar - dians and land-marks The giant moun - tains stand.
help us build up tem - ples And name those tem - ples "home."
CHORUS Dolce with expression
Sing the song that's in your hearts Sing of the great South -
Dolce

west, Thank God, for Ar - i - zon - a In splen-did sun-shine
dressed. For thy beau - ty and thy grand - eur, For thy
re - gal robes so sheen We hail thee Ar - i -
zon - a Our goddess and our queen. Sing the queen.
1.
2.
ff
mf

1
ARIZONA
Words and Music by
REX ALLEN, JR.
Moderately ♩ = 100 M.M.
mf
mp
I love you, Ar- i- zon-a;
Your moun-tains, de- serts and streams;
The rise of Dos Ca-
be- zas* and the out-laws I see in my dreams;
I love you Ar- i-
zon-a, Sup-er- sti-tions and all;
The warmth you

2

ARIZONA

C7 F G7 C7 F F7

give___ at sun- rise; Your sun-sets put mu-sic___ in us all.________

B♭ C7 F Dm B♭ C7 F

Oo,______________________ Ar -________ i- zon-a; You're the ma-gic___ in me;______

B♭ C7 F Dm G7

Oo,___________________ Ar - ________i- zon-a, You're the life-blood of

Gm C7 F C7 F F/A B♭

me; ______________ I love you Ar -_____ i- zon- a; De-sert

* Dos Cabezas (Two Heads) - mountain Peaks in Cochise County Arizona.

3

ARIZONA

C7 F Bb C7 F
dust on the wind; The sage and cac- tus are bloom-ing, and the
G7 C7 F F7 Bb C7 F
smell of the rain on your skin. Oo, Ar- i-
Dm Bb C7 F Bb C7
zon- a; You're the ma-gic in me; Oo,
F Dm G7 Gm7 C7 F
Ar - i- zon-a, you're the life-blood of me;
Ped. *

Arkansas

"Arkansas"

The song "Arkansas," by Mrs. Eva Ware Barnett of Little Rock, was adopted as the official state song by the 41st General Assembly in 1917.

Mrs. Barnett composed "Arkansas" in the Spring of 1916, at the suggestion of Miss Mary McCabe, for use at a New York meeting of the National Federation of Women's Clubs. According to another published account of the song's origin, Mrs. Barnett was encouraged to produce the composition by members of a Little Rock UDC chapter to which she belonged. It was her first musical composition.

When "Arkansas" became the state song in early 1917, it was already in its fourth edition, and some 4,000 copies had been sold. Legal difficulties between the authoress and the state arose in 1940 after the Secretary of State C. G. "Crip" Hall had the preceding year distributed 60,000 free copies of the song to Arkansas schools. On July 26, 1940, Mrs. Barnett filed suit for $3,000 damages, alleging infringement of her copyright privileges. The case came before U.S. District Court in Little Rock, Judge Lemley presiding, on June 25, 1941. Mrs. Barnett claimed that slackened sales as a result of Hall's action had deprived her of her legal royalties of five cents for each copy of the song.

C. G. Hall was principal backer of a move to select a new song which would belong entirely to the state and could be used and distributed freely. In 1947, the General Assembly adopted HCR 17, introduced by Representative Alene Word of Mississippi County. This resolution directed Governor Ben T. Laney to appoint a commission of seven members to select an official state song. The commission was to execute an agreement with the author of the new song that copyright and all other rights should be vested in the state. HCR 17 was adopted by the House on February 6, 1947, and by the Senate on February 19, 1947.

The State Song Commission, headed by Kenneth Osborne of Fayetteville, sponsored a competition. Results were announced on November 20, 1949. The tune selected was the traditional "Arkansas Traveler." Lyrics were a composite production by Mrs. Mabel Bean of Little Rock, Miss Bernice Grantham of Little Rock, Ed Stanfield of Malvern, and T. W. Williamson of Penrose, all of whom shared equally in the $100 prize. First prize of $100 for best march arrangement of the "Traveler" was awarded to Mrs. Virginia Womack Montgomery of Forrest City.

The revamped "Arkansas Traveler" was never popular, particularly in school classrooms, because the fast pace of the old fiddle tune made it difficult to sing. The General Assembly of 1963, by House Concurrent Resolution 16, reestablished "Arkansas" as the state song on condition that Mrs. Barnett assign the copyright to the state. The latter was done, and "Arkansas" has since been the official state song.

History compiled by
Arkansas History Commission.

"Arkansas (You Run Deep in Me)"

"Arkansas (You Run Deep in Me)" was written by Wayland Holyfield. It was adopted as an official song of Arkansas on February 18, 1987.

History compiled by Hladczuk and Hladczuk.

"Oh, Arkansas"

The lyrics to "Oh Arkansas" were written by Terry Rose and Gary Klaff, the music by Gary Klaff and Mark Weinstein.

"Oh, Arkansas" was adopted as an official song of Arkansas on February 18, 1987.

History compiled by Hladczuk and Hladczuk.

"ARKANSAS"

8
I am think - ing to - night of the South-land, Of the
'Tis a land full of joy and of sun - shine, Rich in
home of my child - hood days, Where I roamed through the woods and the
pearls and in dia - monds rare, Full of hope, faith and love for the

mea - dows, By the mill and the brook that plays; Where the
stran - ger Who may pass 'neath her por - tals fair; There the
roses are in bloom, And the sweet magnolia too, Where the jas - mine is white, And the
rice fields are full, And the cot - ton, corn and hay, There the fruits of the field bloom in
fields are vio - let blue, There a wel - come a - waits all her chil - dren Who have
win - ter months and May, 'Tis the land that I love, First of all dear, And to

"Arkansas"

CHORUS
wan - dered a - far from home.
her let us all give cheer.
Ark - an - sas, Ark-an-sas, 'Tis a
name dear, 'Tis the place I call "Home, Sweet Home;" Ark - an -
sas, Ark-ansas, I sa - lute thee, From thy shel - ter no more I'll roam.
8

"Arkansas"

ARKANSAS (YOU RUN DEEP IN ME) WAYLAND HOLYFIELD
PG 1 & 2
VERSE
1. OC-TO-BER MORN-ING IN THE O-ZARK MOUN-TAINS, HILLS A-BLAZ-ING LIKE THAT SUN IN THE SKY. I FELL IN LOVE THERE AND THE FI-RE'S STILL BURN-ING A FLAME THAT NEV-ER WILL DIE.
CHORUS
OH, I MAY WAN-DER, BUT WHEN I DO I WILL NEV-ER BE FAR FROM YOU.
(CONT'D...
© 1985 April Music Inc./Ides of March Music (ASCAP)
49 East 52nd Street; New York, New York 10022
ALL RIGHTS RESERVED INTERNATIONAL COPYRIGHT SECURED

VERSE 2: MOOLIGHT DANCING ON A DELTA LEVEE,
TO A BAND OF FROGS AND WHIPPOORWILL
I LOST MY HEART THERE ONE JULY EVENING

AND IT'S STILL THERE, I CAN TELL.

VERSE 3: MAGNOLIA BLOOMING, MAMA SMILING,

MALLARDS SAILING ON A DECEMBER WIND.
GOD BLESS THE MEMORIES I KEEP RECALLING
LIKE AN OLD FAMILIAR FRIEND.

VERSE 4: AND THERE'S A RIVER RAMBLING THROUGH THE FIELDS AND VALLEYS,
SMOOTH AND STEADY AS SHE MAKES HER WAY SOUTH,
A LOT LIKE THE PEOPLE WHOSE NAME SHE CARRIES.

SHE GOES STRONG AND SHE GOES PROUD.

Lyrics by
Gary Klaff and Terry Rose

Music by
Gary Klaff and Mark Weinstein

Oh, Arkansas

Klaff/Weinstein

Klaff/Weinstein

California

"I Love You, California"

The words and music to "I Love You, California" were written by Los Angelinos F. B. Silverwood and Alfred F. Frankenstein, respectively, in 1913. Mr. Frankenstein was a former conductor of the Los Angeles Symphony Orchestra.

"I Love You, California" was first performed in 1913 by Mary Garden at a concert in the Los Angeles Philharmonic Auditorium and was the official song of both the San Francisco and San Diego Expositions, in 1915. "I Love You, California" was also reported to have been played aboard the first ship that passed through the Panama Canal.

"I Love You, California" became the official state song as the result of Senate Concurrent Resolution 29, which was adopted by the state legislature and then filed with the Office of the Secretary of State on April 26, 1951.

History compiled by Hladczuk and Hladczuk.

2

I LOVE YOU, CALIFORNIA

Words by
F.B. SILVERWOOD

Music by
A.F. FRANKENSTEIN

446-4

fall I love your fer - tile val - leys; your dear
rain I love you, land of flow - ers; land of
jar I love your pur - ple sun - sets, love your
te I love you, Land of Sun - shine, Half your
moun - tains I a - dore I love your grand old
hon - ey, fruit and wine I love you, Cal - i -
skies of a - zure blue I love you, Cal - i -
beau - ties are un - told I loved you in my
o - cean and I love her rug - ged shore.
forn - ia; you have won this heart of mine.
forn - ia; I just can't help lov - ing you.
child - hood, and I'll love you when I'm old.
446-4

Eb
CHORUS (Trio)
Where the snow crowned Gold - en Si -
sempre staccato
f
mf
Gdim
Bb7
er - ras Keep their watch o'er the val - leys bloom, It is
Eb
G7
Cm
C7-5
Bb
C7
F7
there I would be in our land by the sea, Ev - 'ry breeze bear - ing rich per -
446-4

Bb7
Eb
fume, It is here na - ture gives of her rar - est It is
Eb7
Db
Eb7
Ab
C7
Fm
Cdim
Eb
Home Sweet Home to Me, And I know when I die I shall
C7
Fm
F7
Bb7
Eb
breathe my last sigh For my sun - ny Cal - i - forn - ia.
446-4

Colorado

"Where the Columbines Grow"

The State Song of Colorado is reported to be the result of a trip that Dr. Arthur J. Fynn, a prominent educator, took through parts of southwestern Colorado. He and his traveling companions were said to have been so impressed with the beauty of the state that Dr. Fynn was urged to write a song about the "land of the columbines," resulting in "Where the Columbines Grow."

In 1915, the Colorado legislature adopted "Where the Columbines Grow" as the official song of Colorado. The fact that the song makes no explicit reference to the state of Colorado, however, has generated some debate and conflict. Stirring these debates was the introduction of the composition "Hail Colorado," which was a response to the need for a state song that mentions the state name. In 1947, a bill was proposed to make "Hail Colorado" the state song in place of "Where the Columbines Grow." There was an attempt at a compromise to make "Where the Columbines Grow" the official state song and "Hail Colorado" the official state marching song. The compromise bill was passed by the state Senate but was postponed in the House, and thus never reached the governor for his signature.

Ironically, due to a reporting error in the state Senate *Journal*, which identified the bill for "Hail Colorado" as having been passed by both the Senate and the House and signed by the governor, the people of Colorado were led to believe that they had two official songs.

Legally, however, "Where the Columbines Grow" is the only "official" state song.

History compiled by Hladczuk and Hladczuk.

Where The Columbines Grow

A. J. FYNN

Printed in the U. S. A.

rit.

wild foam-ing wa-ters dash on - - ward To-ward lands where the
home of the wolf is de - sert - - ed, The an - te - lope
clo - ver be-deck the green mead - - ow, In days when the

a tempo

trop - ic stars shine;____ Where the scream of the bold moun - tain
moans for his dead,____ The war - whoop re - ech - oes no
o - ri - oles sing,____ Let the gold - en - rod her - ald the

Piu mosso

ea - gle____ Re-sponds to the notes of the dove____ Is the
lon - ger,____ The In - di - an's on - ly a name,____ And the
au - tumn;____ But, un - der the mid - sum-mer sky,____ In its

Where The C. G. 4

SOPRANO *a tempo* *accel.*

'Tis the land where the columbines grow, ___ Over looking the plains far below, ___ While the

ALTO *a tempo*

'Tis the land where the columbines grow, ___ Over looking the plains far below, ___ While the

TENOR *a tempo*

'Tis the land where the columbines, columbines grow, Over looking the plains far below, far below, While the

BASS *a tempo*

'Tis the land where the columbines grow, ___ Over looking the plains far below, ___ While the

a tempo

mf

rit.

cool summer breeze in the ev-er-green trees Soft-ly sings where the col-um-bines grow. ___

rit.

cool summer breeze in the ev-er-green trees Soft-ly sings where the col-um-bines grow. ___

rit.

cool summer breeze in the ev-er-green trees Soft-ly sings where the col-um-bines grow. ___

rit.

cool summer breeze in the ev-er-green trees Soft-ly sings where the col-um-bines grow. ___

rit.

Connecticut

"Yankee Doodle"

When the French and Indian War broke out in 1755, Colonel Thomas Fitch of Norwalk, Connecticut, held command over several companies of volunteers who entered the service at their own expense. When a call for reinforcements went out, Colonel Fitch and his ragged regiment prepared to march. Legend has it that Fitch's sister Betty, appalled at the motley appearance of the men, ran to the chicken coop and returned with feathers stating, "Put these in your hat, soldiers should wear plumes." As the regiment approached Albany, Richard Schuckberg, a surgeon in one of the New York companies of the British Army, watched the Connecticut Fourth Militia pass by. When he saw the troops, clad in every imaginable outfit and with the chicken feathers in their tricorn hats, he jotted down a new verse to what he knew as the Dutch version of "Yankee Doodle." During the American Revolution, the song gained popularity with the patriots. It was reportedly played as British General Burgoyne surrendered to General Gates in 1777 at Saratoga and as Cornwallis surrendered to General Washington in 1781 at Yorktown.

"Yankee Doodle" was adopted as an official song of Connecticut on October 1, 1978.

History courtesy of the Connecticut State Library, State Archives Division.

Unexpurgated version pub. in England about 1780

YANKEE DOODLE, or
(as now Christened by the SAINTS of New England)
THE LEXINGTON MARCH

NB. The Words to be Sung thro' the Nose, & in the West Country drawl & dialect.

Sk:

This is the first sheet music ed. found extant

7

American National Song

Yankee Doodle.

Delaware

"Our Delaware"

The poem, "Our Delaware," by George B. Hynson (born near Milford, Delaware, on April 3, 1862), was set to music composed by William M. S. Brown (born at Wilmington, Delaware, on May 16, 1860). It was officially adopted as the State Song of Delaware on April 7, 1925.

In recent years, the use of the song has been limited and the construction of the poem appeared to be a contributing factor. It consists of three stanzas—one for each county, New Castle, Kent, and Sussex.

After consultation with state officials, the Director of Music Education, Floyd T. Hart, sent letters to forty educational and community organizations suggesting the selection of an additional stanza applying to the state as a whole. This stanza would be used either alone or with a county stanza.

When this suggestion received a strong endorsement, permission was requested from the 120th General Assembly to select the additional stanza. This was granted by House Joint Resolution No. 5, and the Governor was authorized to appoint a selection committee. From the ninety-five stanzas received by the committee, the one submitted by Donn Devine was approved on May 23, 1960.

The House Joint Resolution further stated that "the stanza selected by the committee will be made available on a trial basis to schools and organizations in communities throughout the State."

History courtesy of the Delaware State Archives.

OUR DELAWARE.

Words by GEO. B. HYNSON. **Music by WILL M. S. BROWN.**

Moderato.

1. Oh the hills of dear New Cas - tle, And the smil - ing vales be - tween, When the corn is all in tas - sel, And the mead - ow lands are green; Where the cat - tle crop the clo - ver, And its breath is in the air, While the

2. Where the wheat fields break and bil - low, In the peace-ful land of Kent, Where the toil - er seeks his pil - low, With the bless - ings of con - tent; Where the bloom that tints the peach - es, Cheeks of mer - ry maid-ens share, And the

3. Dear old Sus - sex vis - sions lin - ger, Of the hol - ly and the pine, Of Hen - lo - pens Jew - eled fing - er, Flash - ing out a-cross the brine; Of the gar - dens and the hed - ges, And the wel - come wait-ing there, For the

* From New Cas - tle's rol - ling mead - ows, Through the fair rich fields of Kent, To the Sus - sex shores hear ech - oes, Of the pledge we now pre - sent: Lib - er - ty and In - de pen - dence, We will guard with loy - al care, And hold

mf

* *New Stanza authorized by the 120th General Assembly on a trial basis. Words by Donn Devine chosen by selection committee.*

sun is shin - ing o - ver Our be - lov - ed Del - a - ware.
wood land cho - rus preach - es A re - joice - ing Del - a - ware.
loy - al son that pledg - es Faith to good old Del - a - ware.
fast to free - dom's pres - ence, In our home state Del - a - ware.
CHORUS Tempo di March.
Oh, our Del - a - ware! Our be - lov - ed Del - a-ware! For the sun is shin-ing
mf
o- ver our be - lov - ed Del - a - ware, Oh! our Del -a - ware! Our be-lov-ed
rall.
Del - a-ware! Heres the loy - al son that pledg-es, Faith to good old Del - a - ware.
8va
rall.

Florida

"Old Folks at Home"

Composed in Pittsburgh and published in New York in October 1851, this was undoubtedly Foster's most popular song and the one that earned him (and later his widow and daughter) the largest royalties from sheet-music sales. It is the song that is perhaps most immediately associated with the composer's name. A long-noted irony in this respect is that Foster's name did not appear during his lifetime on the published song. (His name did appear as composer after the copyright of the song was renewed in 1879.) It was of course Edwin P. Christy who was credited as having "written and composed" "Old Folks at Home," and Foster himself was responsible for this. He apparently sold to Christy the right to be publicized as composer of the song for the sum of $5.00. Eight months after "Old Folks" appeared, Foster regretted his action and tried unsuccessfully to nullify the agreement.

The plantation scene of Foster's celebration of the good life among the old folks was originally set on the Pedee River. Drafts of the poem in his manuscript workbook read:

Way down upon de Pedee ribber
Far far away

and then:

Swanee
Way down upon de ~~Pedee~~ ribber
Far far away.

He perhaps decided to use the two-syllable corruption of Florida's Suawnee because the initial vowel is more graceful for singing. It is difficult to imagine what subsequent generations of Tin Pan Alley lyricists would have done without the corrupt but musical Suawnee to fall back on. The word eventually served almost as well as the mythical Dixie to conjure a stereotyped Southern setting.

History source: Richard Jackson, ed., *Popular Songs of Nineteenth Century America* (New York: Dover Publications, 1976).

Old Folks At Home.

(Suawnee River.)

Words & Music by
STEPHEN C. FOSTER.

509-3

Century Music Publishing Company

New York

Edited Edition

When programming or performing this number on the air, kindly give credit to the Century Edition.

3
turn - in' eb - ber, Dere's whar de ole folks stay.
days I squan-der'd, Ma - ny de songs I sung.
mem - 'ry rush - es, No mat - tah whar I rove.
All up an down de whole cre - a - tion Sad - ly I roam,
When I was play - in' wid my brud-der, Hap - py was I,
When will I see de bees a - hum-min' All roun' de comb?
rit.
rit.
Still long - in' foh de ole plan - ta - tion An' foh de ole folks at home.
Oh! take me to mah kind ole mud - der, Dere let me lib an die.
When will I heah de ban - jo tum-min' Down in my good ole home.
rit.
rit.
Old folks at home. 509-3

Old folks at home. 509-3

Georgia

"Georgia on My Mind"

One of the better trivia questions in the music business is: who wrote the lyrics to "Georgia on My Mind?" The answer is Stuart Gorrell, and he and my father, Hoagy Carmichael, wrote the song in 1930 almost as a lark, and with the help of some pretty good Scotch. The inspiration was theirs; the booze was borrowed.

Dad went to Indiana University, and one of his best college chums was Stuart Gorrell. Carmichael was going to be a lawyer and Gorrell, when not hanging around the local "jazz joint" (called The Book Nook!) had promised someone that he would eventually be a success in the world of business. As dad told the story, the two of them were together at a party in New York and dad played what he had of the "Georgia" music line for Gorrell and some friends. After the party broke up, the two of them went back to a friend's apartment and worked on the tune throughout the night. Stu wrote what he thought would be a good lyric line on the back of a post card (now displayed in the Carmichael Room at Indiana University) and showed it to dad. One can still plainly see the few, but important, changes that Carmichael made on that small piece of cardboard to Gorrell's lyrical scratchings. The song was improved upon, and the lyrics written, in that boozy early morning, and recorded in September by a band that included dad's great friend, Bix Beiderbecke—a recording session that proved to be Bix's last.

Dad went on to write many more songs, some of them hits, and Stu Gorrell kept his promise and became a Vice President at Chase Bank. Gorrell never tried to write another song lyric, but "Georgia" became a hit after the war and dad, true to his word—although Gorrell was not legally credited as the lyricist by the music publisher—always sent Stu a check for what would have been his share of royalty. The royalty income from that song is substantial and, after Stu died, the income put his daughter through college.

Dad's sister, also named "Georgia," always thought that dad had her in mind when he wrote that song. I remember the smile on her brother's face when she would, usually in the presence of company and with the help of some refreshment, draw attention to that fact. It doesn't matter . . . but maybe Frankie Trumbauer said it best when he was trying to talk dad into writing a song called "Georgia": "Nobody lost much [money] writing about the South."

History courtesy of Hoagy B. Carmichael, Jr.

GEORGIA ON MY MIND

Lyric by STUART GORRELL
Piano Arrangement by HOAGY CARMICHAEL
Music by HOAGY CARMICHAEL

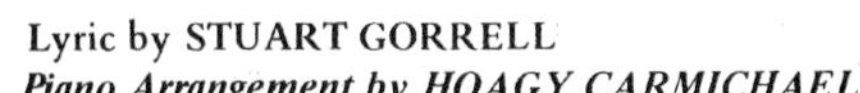

Introduction : *Rubato* **p** *two trumpet salute*

Verse :

Eb G7 Bbdim C7

Mel - o - dies bring mem-o - ries, mem'-ries of a

p *Expressive*

F7 Fdim Eb G7 Cm

song, a song that sings of Geor- gia,

f

F9 F7 E7 Eb6 Bb7

back where I be - long.

ritardando

Georgia On My Mind - 4 - 1
1443GSMX - 4 - 1

Georgia On My Mind · 4 · 2
1443GSMX · 4 · 2

4
Cm6 Fm6 Cm7 A♭9 Cm6 A♭dim
Oth- er arms reach out to me, oth - er eyes smile
Cm7 F9 Cm Cm (B♭ Bass) Cm (A♭ Bass) G7 Cm7 D7
ten der - ly, still in peace - ful dreams I see the
f
Gm A7 D7-9 Gm Fm (B♭ Bass) E♭
road leads back to you. (you.) Geor- gia,
G7 Cm Cm7 F A♭dim D7 E♭ D7
To Coda
Geor-gia, no peace I find, just an old sweet song keeps
Georgia On My Mind · 4 · 3
1443GSMX · 4 · 3

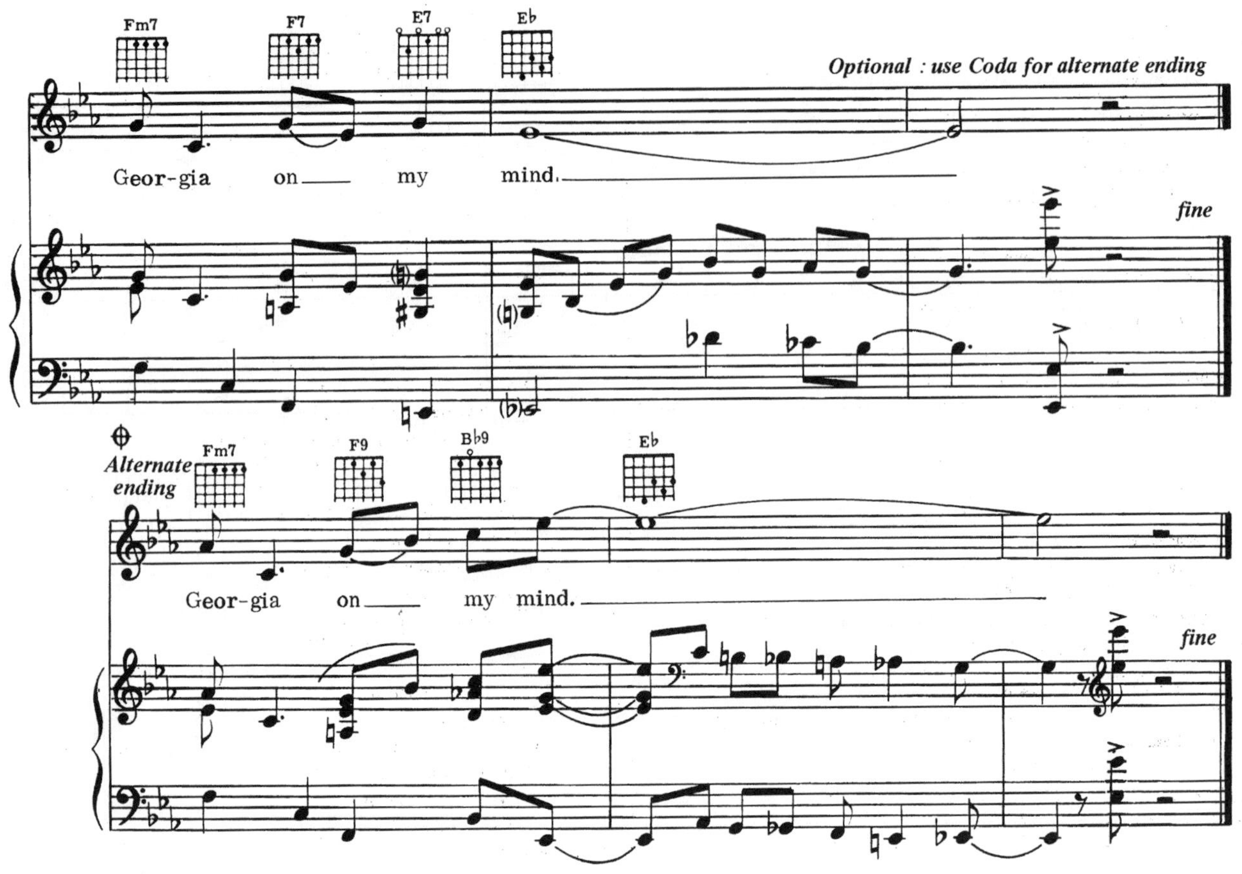

Melodies bring memories
That linger in my heart.
Make me think of Georgia,
Why did we ever part?
Some sweet day when blossoms fall
And all the world's a song,
I'll go back to Georgia,
'Cause that's where I belong.

Hawaii

"Hawaii Ponoi"

This was Hawaii's former national anthem and is now its state song. King David Kalākaua composed the text in 1874 to the tune of "God Save the King" as a hymn to Kamehameha I. Henry Berger composed the music shortly afterwards. There is some musical resemblance to "God Save the King" in "Hawaii Ponoi," especially in the meter, rhythmic patterns, general phrasing, and melodic movement. The arrangement for four-part chorus and band is impressive in the grand manner of the majestic anthems of European royalty.

The anthem was first sung by the Kawaiahaʻo Choir on the birthday of King Kalākaua, November 16, 1874. Subsequently it became the regular closing piece for every Royal Hawaiian Band performance. In 1876 it was proclaimed the national anthem of the Kingdom of Hawaiʻi. Even after the U.S. annexation, the song was popularly accepted as the Territory's "national" anthem. In 1967, the Hawaiʻi State Legislature passed an act making it the state song.

"Hawaii Ponoi" is not sung and played today as frequently as it was in the past, although it is still performed regularly by the Royal Hawaiian Band and the Kamehameha Schools' choirs. "Hawaii Aloha," Lorenzo Lyons's patriotic hymn, is often sung today in place of "Hawaii Ponoi."

History source: George S. Kanahele, ed., *Hawaiian Music and Musicians: An Illustrated History* (Honolulu: University Press of Hawaii, 1979).

48

HAWAII PONOI

Hawaiian National Anthem

* Spear or lance

Idaho

"Here We Have Idaho"

The music for the Idaho state song, composed by Sallie Hume-Douglas, was copyrighted on November 4, 1915, under the title "Garden of Paradise."

In 1917, McKinley Helm, a student at the University of Idaho, wrote the verse which became the chorus of the Idaho state song, and Alice Bessee set the words to the music by Sallie Hume-Douglas. The song was popular then, and Alice Bessee had no idea of its origin. This song won the annual University prize for that year, and eventually became the University alma mater.

Bethel Packenham, a student from Boise at the University from 1928 to 1932, provided new verses for the alma mater; and about the same time, Albert J. Tompkins, Director of Music in the Boise Public Schools, wrote still another set of verses for the song. The University obtained permission from Mrs. Douglas, by a contract executed January 2, 1930, to use the melody forever. Then the next year, by act of March 11, 1931, the Idaho legislature designated "Here We Have Idaho," previously known at the University as "Our Idaho," as the Idaho state song. The statute did not identify the words to be used, but the verses published in the *House Journal*, February 24, 1931, are the Tompkins-Helm verses. These verses came from the University, and there is some indication they were in use there before the Packenham verses were. The Tompkins verses are more appropriate for a state song, while the Packenham verses are an alma mater.

Original McKinley Helm version: "Our Idaho."

Words by McKinley Helm, 1917; Music, Garden of Paradise, by Mrs. Sallie Hume Douglas, as arranged by Alice Bessee.

A pioneer state built a college to share.
Its youth and its rigorous life
That flourished and grew from year to year,
Beset by political strife.

Then fire came destroying the child of the state,
But quickly she sprang up anew.
Upon the ashes that marked where the old
Had 'eft a bold spirit that grew.

And now on a hill that is searched by the winds,
There stands in security,
Proud of her youth and a pioneer still,
A staunch University.

CHORUS
And here we have Idaho,
Scourged on her way to fame,
Silver and gold in the sunlight blaze,
And romance lies in her name.

Singing, we're singing of you,
Ah, proudly, too,
All our lives thru, we'll go
Singing, singing of you, Alma Mater,
Our Idaho.

History courtesy of the Idaho Historical Society.

HERE WE HAVE IDAHO

Official Idaho State Song by Enactment of Twenty-first Session of Idaho Legislature.

Words by McKinley Helm — Music by Sallie Hume-Douglas

You've heard of the wonders our land does possess
Its beautiful valleys and hills;
The majestic forests where nature abounds,
We love every nook and rill.

There's only one state in this great land of ours,
Where ideals can be realized;
The pioneers made it so for you and me,
A legacy we'll always prize.

CHORUS

And here we have Idaho,
Winning her way to fame;
Silver and gold in the sunlight blaze,
And romance lies in her name;

Singing, we're singing of you,
Ah, proudly, too, All our lives thru,
We'll go singing, singing of you,
Singing of Idaho.

Printed in U.S.A. — State of Idaho, Bureau of Printing Services

Illinois

"Illinois"

The song "Illinois," by act of the 54th General Assembly, became the official state song on June 30, 1925. Senator Florence Fifer Bohrer, of Bloomington, daughter of former Governor Fifer, and the first woman to serve as a member of the state Senate, introduced the bill. The bill passed unopposed in both houses and was signed into law by Governor Small.

The song, written by Charles H. Chamberlin, had been the unofficial state song for many years. Adapting the melody from a song titled "Baby Mine," written about 1870 by Archibald Johnston and Charles Mackay, Chamberlin wrote the "Illinois" words sometime between 1890 and 1894 for Mr. Chamberlin's friend, Colonel O. B. Knight, in connection with the plans for securing the World's Columbian Exposition (the World's Fair) for the city of Chicago.

It was first sung at a reunion of the Army of the Potomac, in Chicago. Former President William McKinley, toastmaster at the reunion, congratulated Chamberlin on writing a song "that will never die." Colonel Knight continued to sing the song throughout Illinois and Washington, D.C.

Charles H. Chamberlin was born of Scotch-English parentage in Elba, New York. He enlisted in the Regular Army when he was 18 years old and was one of General Sike's Regulars at the opening of the Civil War. He fought in the first and second battles of Bull Run, the siege of Richmond, Fair Oaks, and was then wounded at Gaines' Mill. Mr. Chamberlin was hospital steward during the last two years of his military service at Fortress Monroe, Virginia, in the Medical Directors' Office under Dr. Eli McClellen.

Chamberlin died on September 16, 1894. The third verse of the song "Illinois" is engraved on his headstone in Forest Home Cemetery in Chicago.

History compiled by Sharon S. Hladczuk.

ILLINOIS
(BY THY RIVERS GENTLY FLOWING)

Words by CHARLES H. CHAMBERLIN
New Verses by WIN STRACKE

Music by ARCHIBALD JOHNSON
Arr. by NORMAN LUBOFF

Indiana

"On the Banks of the Wabash, Far Away"

I [Theodore Dreiser] recall being with him when he composed "On the Banks of the Wabash," which has now been adopted by Paul's native state as its state song. In an almost unintentional way I had a hand in that, and it has always cheered me to think I had, although I never had the least talent for musical composition or song versification. It was one of those delightful summer Sunday mornings (1896) and we had gone over to the office to do a little work.

"What do you suppose would make a good song these days?" he asked in an idle, meditative mood, sitting at the piano and thrumming while I, at a nearby table, was examining some magazines. "Why don't you give me an idea once in a while?"

"Why don't you write something about a state or a river?" I retorted. "Look at 'My Old Kentucky Home,' 'Dixie,' 'Old Black Joe'—why don't you do something like that? Take Indiana, what's the matter with it—the Wabash River? It's as good as any other river, and you were 'raised' beside it."

I smile now when I recall the apparent zest with which he at once seized on this. "That's not a bad idea," he agreed. "Why don't you write the words and let me put the music to them? We'll do it together."

"But I can't," I replied. "I don't know how to do these things. You write it. I'll help, maybe."

After a little urging, however, I took a piece of paper and scribbled in the most tentative manner the first verse and chorus of that song almost as it was published. I think one or two lines were too long or didn't rhyme, and eventually he hammered them into shape. He read it, insisted that it was fine, and that I should do a second verse, something with a story in it—a girl, perhaps, a task which I solemnly rejected.

Some time later, disagreeing with him—my fault, I am sure—I left. Time passed and I heard nothing. One Spring night, however, the following year, as I was lying in bed trying to sleep, I heard a quartette of boys in the distance. At first I could not make out the words, but the melody attracted my attention. It was plaintive and compelling. I listened, attracted, satisfied that it was a new popular success that had "caught on." As they drew near my window I heard the words, "On the Banks of the Wabash" most mellifluously harmonized.

I jumped up. A part of the words were mine—my careless, indifferent gift to him. But made by his melody and labor into something so much more appealing than I could ever have imagined. It was Paul's song—my very successful and admirable brother. He had another "hit" then. And they were already singing it in the street. In three months more it was everywhere—in the papers, on the stage, on the street-organs, played by orchestras, bands, whistled and sung every place.

"On the Banks of the Wabash" became Indiana's official state song by Act of the Indiana General Assembly on March 14, 1913.

History included by permission of the Dreiser Trust.

Respectfully inscribed to Miss Mary E. South, Terre Haute, Indiana.

ON THE BANKS OF THE WABASH, FAR AWAY.

SONG and CHORUS.

Words and Music by PAUL DRESSER.

231

times my tho'ts re - vert to scenes of child - hood, Where I
there I tried to tell her that I loved her, It was
first re - ceived my les - sons - Na - ture's school, ... But
there I begged of her to be my bride, ... Long
one thing there is miss - ing in the pict - ure, With
years have passed since I strolled thro' the church - yard, She's

rall.
out her face it seems so in - com - plete, ... I
sleep - ing there my an - gel Ma - ry dear, ... I
rall.
long to see my moth - er in the door - way, As she
loved her but she thought I did - 'nt mean it, Still I'd
a tempo.
rall. p
stood there years a - go, her boy to greet. . . . .
give my fu - ture were she on - ly here. . . . .
rall. p

CHORUS.
mp Espressivo.
Oh, the moon-light's fair to-night a-long the Wa - bash, From the
mp
fields there comes the breath of new-mown hay, ... Through the
syc - a-mores the can - dle lights are gleam - ing, On the
banks of the Wa-bash, far a - way. . . . .
pp
D.C.

Iowa

"The Song of Iowa"

The state song of Iowa, entitled "The Song of Iowa," written by S. H. M. Byers in 1867, was at that time, and has been, sung to the tune of the old German song "O Tannenbaum". This song, however, set to a different melody by Paul Lange, was published by Bollman and Schatzman, St. Louis, Missouri, in 1867.

Byers received the inspiration for writing this production while he was confined in Libby Prison, at Richmond, Virginia, after he had been taken by the enemy in the battle of Lookout Mountain, in 1863. His captors were accustomed to pass by his prison playing the air of "O Tannenbaum" or "My Maryland," or singing it "set to Southern and bitter words." It was at this time that Byers resolved to put that tune "to loyal words." The song "Iowa" was the crystallization of his resolve. This musical composition was authorized to be recognized as the state song of Iowa by a House Concurrent Resolution of the Senate on March 20, 1911. The resolution reads:

> Whereas, the patriotic song of Iowa by S.H.M. Byers, has, for years, been sung in all the schools of the State, and on thousands of public occasions, political and social, and wherever Iowa people come together in other States.
>
> Therefore, Be it Resolved by the House, the Senate concurring, that it be hereby declared to be recognized as the State Song.

The theme of Byers's lyric centers on his love for, and praise of Iowa, the cornfields, prairies, purple sunsets, fair women, and the patriotic sons of his beloved state.

History courtesy of the
State Historical Society of Iowa.

The Song of Iowa.

By S. H. M. BYERS.

3 And she has maids whose laughing eyes,
Iowa, O! Iowa,
To him who loves were Paradise,
Iowa, O! Iowa.
O! happiest fate that e'er was known,
Such eyes to shine for one alone,
To call such beauty all his own,
Iowa, O! Iowa.

4 Go read the story of thy past,
Iowa, O! Iowa,
What glorious deeds, what fame thou hast!
Iowa, O! Iowa.
So long as time's great cycle runs,
Or nations weep their fallen ones,
Thou'lt not forget thy patriot sons,
Iowa, O! Iowa.

* "*Der Tannenbaum,*" the old air to which this song is sung, was a popular German Students' song as early as 1819. It had been a Volks song long before that, even. During our Civil War, the Southerners adapted it to the song "My Maryland."

Kansas

"Home on the Range"

The words of the Kansas state song were written in 1873 by Dr. Brewster Higley in his one-room dugout on the banks of the Beaver River. The pioneer of Smith County, Kansas, Dr. Higley (1823–1911) was known as a "writing" doctor who practiced medicine and wrote poetry.

The music was composed by Daniel E. Kelley when he was 30 years old. Kelley (1843–1905) was born in North Kingston, Rhode Island, but moved to Kansas in 1872 and settled at Gaylord. He was extremely popular as an entertainer and with his wife, Lulu Harlan, and the Harlan orchestra (composed of her brothers Clarence and Eugene), he performed for dances and celebrations, traveling to various parts of the country. One of the songs that he played was a song then known as "Western Home" but that became known as "Home on the Range."

Dr. Higley's poem "Western Home" was published in the *Kerwin Chief*, a Kansas newspaper, on March 21, 1874. On February 3, 1876, the same poem was printed in another newspaper, the *Stockton News*, under the title "My Home in the West" by Mrs. Emma Race of Raceburgh in Rooks County, Kansas. The editor of the *Kerwin Chief* recognized the poem as that of Dr. Higley, and on February 26, 1876, he reprinted "Western Home" under the headline "PLAGIARISM." This record of plagiarism occurred shortly after the Harlan orchestra was formed, but it was the first of many plagiarisms to be documented later on.

According to Kirke Mechem in the November 1949 issue of the *Kansas Historical Quarterly*, if it weren't for plagiarism, neither Higley nor Kelley would have gotten recognition for their song. Indeed, there were a number of people who claimed authorship (or had it claimed for them) of the song that became a folk song known and sung virtually around the world. At its peak, the ballad was often listened to by President Franklin D. Roosevelt at the White House, and he frequently led guests in singing "Home on the Range." This stamp of approval helped to make the song one of the nation's hit songs, and by 1934 it was a top radio hit for six months.

People in the music business had a field day, for there was no copyright and no one knew who the author was. Then a 1934 lawsuit virtually stopped the music. Mary and William Goodwin of Tempe, Arizona, said they had written the words and music of a song titled "An Arizona Home," copyrighted in 1905, and claimed that their song was the parent song of "Home on the Range."

The Music Publishers Protective Association hired Samuel Moanfeldt, a New York attorney, to research the origins of the words and music of "Home on the Range." After months of investigation, interviewing people, and getting affidavits as evidence, he revealed how the song had spread from one singer to another, without printed words or music, until it was well known on the Western Frontier.

Moanfeldt discovered that John Lomax, a collector of folk music, had researched cowboy songs, and that all popular versions of the song could be traced to a 1910 book titled *Cowboy Songs*. The words changed—from the specific descriptions of Dr. Higley's Kansas to more general verses relating to life on the range—as the song became a cowboy's ballad.

A year before the song was written, the Santa Fe Railroad reached Dodge City, Kansas, and almost overnight Dodge City became the largest cattle market in the world and the Southwest's shipping center. Mechem attributes the song's popularity to being helped by that occurrence. Through the convergence of trade, the song was brought to other parts of the country. Moanfeldt went to Dodge City and got signed statements from ex-cowboys and others who said the song was well known in the cow camps prior to 1890. There were various versions of the song, and it was even claimed by Colorado as "Colorado Home."

Moanfeldt's affidavits convinced critics that "Home on the Range," being written in Kansas and being about Kansas, belonged to Kansas, but it took 12 years to make it the official state song. In 1947, the Kansas legislature officially adopted "Home on the Range" as the state song with verses in the bill from Mrs. Cal Harlan, who had written them out from memory a few years before; they differ only a little from the versions published in 1876 in the *Kerwin Chief* and in the reprint of an 1873 issue of the *Smith County Pioneer* published in 1914. The Harlan version, as it is referred to, is a fourth version of the song, which was modified over 37 years of folk singing. The comparison of the versions, along with Samuel Moanfeldt's report of his investigation, is found in Mechem's article.

History compiled by Sharon S. Hladczuk.

A HOME ON THE RANGE*

Oscar J. Fox, San Antonio, Texas, published an arrangement of this song after it had remained unnoticed for many years in *Cowboy Songs*. For a time "Home on the Range" was the most popular song on the air. A suit for a half-million dollars was brought on copyright—probably the largest sum ever asked for one song. A Negro saloon keeper in San Antonio gave me the music to "Home on the Range" as herein reprinted. The words are also identical with the version of *Cowboy Songs*, 1910. They were assembled from several sources and have since often been pirated.

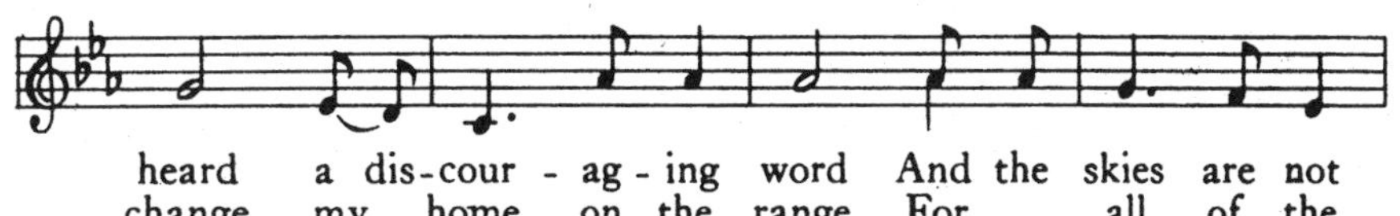

Cowboy Songs and Other Frontier Ballads

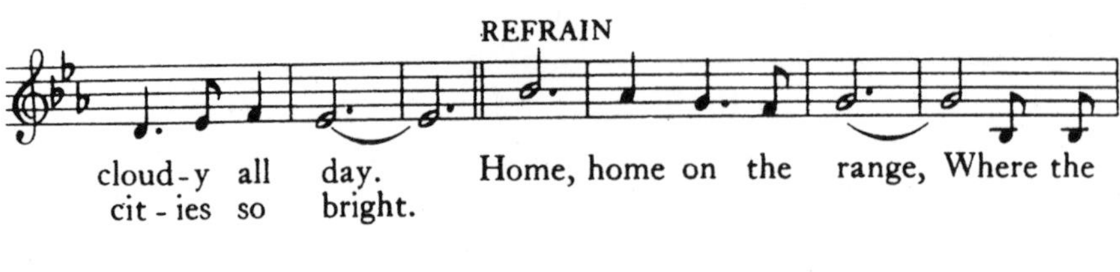

Oh, give me a home where the buffalo roam,
Where the deer and the antelope play,
Where seldom is heard a discouraging word
And the skies are not cloudy all day.

> Home, home on the range,
> Where the deer and the antelope play;
> Where seldom is heard a discouraging word
> And the skies are not cloudy all day.

Where the air is so pure, the zephyrs so free,
The breezes so balmy and light,
That I would not exchange my home on the range
For all the cities so bright.

The red man was pressed from this part of the West,
He's likely no more to return
To the banks of Red River where seldom if ever
Their flickering campfires burn.

[425]

Kentucky

"My Old Kentucky Home"

Stephen Foster composed this song probably in 1852, and it was published in January 1853. There are several legends that connect the piece to Federal Hill, the summer home of Judge John Rowan in Bardstown, Kentucky, but there is no documentary evidence from the period to prove that Foster had much connection with the place. Judge Rowan, a one time U.S. Senator from Kentucky, was a cousin of Stephen's father and well known to the Foster family. Stephen probably visited Federal Hill in the 1840s, but it is most unlikely that he composed "My Old Kentucky Home" there or that he even had the house in mind when he composed it.

Foster's manuscript workbook reveals that the original title of the poem was "Poor Uncle Tom, Good Night" and that the text varied from that of the final published version. Each verse originally ended with the line "Den poor Uncle Tom, good night." Foster was perhaps inspired by Harriet Beecher Stowe's recently published *Uncle Tom's Cabin* (1851) or was attempting to capitalize on the book's new fame. In any case, legends die hard, and Federal Hill is still secure in Foster lore and is a museum and tourist attraction. Kentucky took the song as its own long ago and finally proclaimed it the official state song in 1928.

History source: Richard Jackson, ed., *Popular Songs of Nineteenth Century America* (New York: Dover Publications, 1976).

MY OLD KENTUCKY HOME, GOOD-NIGHT!

Words and Music by

STEPHEN C. FOSTER.

corn top's ripe and the meadow's in the bloom While the birds make music all the
day. The young folks roll on the lit_tle cabin floor, All
merry, all happy and bright: By'n by Hard Times comes a
knocking at the door, Then my old Kentucky Home, good night!

CHORUS

Tenor.

Weep no more, my lady, oh! weep no more to_ day! We will sing one song For the

AIR. 1st Soprano.

2d Soprano.

Weep no more, my lady, oh! weep no more to_ day! We will sing one song For the

Bass.

old Kentucky Home, For the old Kentucky Home, far a_ way.

old Kentucky Home, For the old Kentucky Home, far a_ way.

2d. V.
They hunt no more for the possum and the coon On the meadow, the hill and the shore, They
sing no more by the glimmer of the moon, On the bench by the old cabin door. The
day goes by like a shadow o'er the heart, With sorrow where all was de_light: The
time has come when the darkies have to part, Then my old Kentucky Home, good-night! Chorus.
3d. V.
The head must bow and the back will have to bend, Wherever the darkey may go: A
few more days, and the trouble all will end In the field where the sugar-canes grow. A
few more days for to tote the weary load, No matter 'twill never be light, A
few more days till we totter on the road, Then my old Kentucky Home, good-night! Chorus.
Quidor Engr.

Louisiana

"Give Me Louisiana"

"Give Me Louisiana" was written by Miss Doralice Fontane of Baton Rouge, Louisiana. Miss Fontane not only taught music but also was an entertainer and composer. Among her better known compositions are "Let's March Together, People of the World," and "March on! America."

"Give Me Louisiana" was adopted as an official state song, by Act 431, in 1970.

Unfortunately, because all attempts to ascertain ownership and/or copyright have been to no avail, neither the music nor the lyrics have been reproduced in this volume.

"You Are My Sunshine"

"You Are My Sunshine" was written by Charles Mitchell and former, two-term Louisiana governor Jimmie Davis.

"You Are My Sunshine" was adopted as an official state song, by Act 540, in 1977.

History compiled by Hladczuk and Hladczuk.

YOU ARE MY SUNSHINE

Words and Music by
JIMMIE DAVIS and
CHARLES MITCHELL

You Are My Sunshine - 2 - 1
4549YSMX - 2 - 1

3
F
C7
F
tak - en and I hung my head and cried:
oth - er you'll re - gret it all some day:
oth - er you have shat - tered all my dreams:
Chorus
F
F dim.
F
F7
Bb
YOU ARE MY SUN - SHINE my on - ly sun - shine you make me hap - py
F
F7
Bb
F
when skies are gray You'll nev - er know dear how much I love you Please don't
C7
1-2. F
3.
take my sun - shine a - way.
2. I'll al - ways
3. You told me
way.
rit.
You Are My Sunshine - 2 - 2
4549YSMX - 2 - 2

Maine

"State of Maine Song"

In 1931, the Maine Publicity Bureau conducted a contest in order to find a state song. Of the 116 songs submitted for consideration, the Bureau chose "State of Maine Song," words and music by an attorney, Roger Vinton Snow, of Portland, Maine.

Mr. Snow graduated from Williams College in 1912, after which he attended Harvard Law School, graduating in 1915.

The 86th Legislature, in 1933, voted the "State of Maine Song" the official song of the state of Maine.

History compiled by Hladczuk and Hladczuk.

2

State of Maine Song

Words and Music by
ROGER VINTON SNOW

3
land, To shout your prais-es till the ech-oes ring.
Should fate un - kind send
us to roam The scent of the fra-grant pines, the

4
tang of the salt-y sea will call us home.
CHORUS
p-f Oh Pine Tree State Your
p-f
woods, fields and hills, Your
lakes, streams and rock - bound coast will ev - er fill our

5
hearts with thrills
And tho' we seek far and
wide
Our search will be in vain
To find a fair - er spot on earth than
Maine! Maine! Maine!
cresc.
staccato
in strict tempo
1
2

Maryland

"Maryland, My Maryland!"

This was one of the most popular rallying songs in the Confederacy during the Civil War, rivaling "Dixie" as "the song of the Southern people." The words were written by the Baltimore poet James Ryder Randall (1839–1908) in April 1861 at Poydras College near New Roads, Louisiana. He read in the *New Orleans Delta* the account of Massachusetts troops being fired upon as they passed through Baltimore; one of Randall's friends was the first casualty when the Union soldiers returned fire. "I had long been absent from my native city," the poet later recounted, "and the startling event there inflamed my mind. That night I could not sleep. . . . I proceeded to write the song of 'My Maryland.' . . . The whole poem of nine stanzas as originally written, was dashed off rapidly, when once begun."

The tune of "Maryland, My Maryland!" is that of a German folksong first published in 1799. It is also well known in its use with two other poems, the German carol "O Tannenbaum" and the college song "Lauriger Horatius." Jennie Cary, member of a prominent Confederate-activist family in Baltimore, conceived the idea of using the old tune with Randall's poem shortly after it appeared in the Baltimore press. Miss Cary also introduced the song to a mass audience under dramatic circumstances. She was one in a small party permitted to visit General P.G.T. Beauregard near Fairfax County Court House, Virginia, in July 1861 shortly after the first battle of Manassas. In darkness she stood before a tent and performed the stirring song for Beauregard's troops, who gradually joined in the refrain.

The musical setting was first published by the Baltimore firm Miller & Beacham in October 1861. The first edition carries no attribution of authorship, only stating that it was "Written by A Baltimorean in Louisiana." The musical adaptation is credited to an anonymous "C. E." (probably Charles Ellerbrock, a soldier-composer whose name appears in later editions as arranger). Randall does receive credit in the first Confederate edition published in January 1862 by A. E. Blackmar & Bro., a leading New Orleans firm that subsequently brought out other songs by Randall. This edition also carries the credit "Music by a Lady of Baltimore," apparently referring to Jennie Cary.

History source: Richard Jackson, ed., *Popular Songs of Nineteenth Century America* (New York: Dover Publications, 1976).

Andante.

I. The despot's heel is on thy shore, Ma-ry-land, My Ma-ry-land! His touch is at thy temple door, Ma-ry-land, My Ma-ry-land! A-

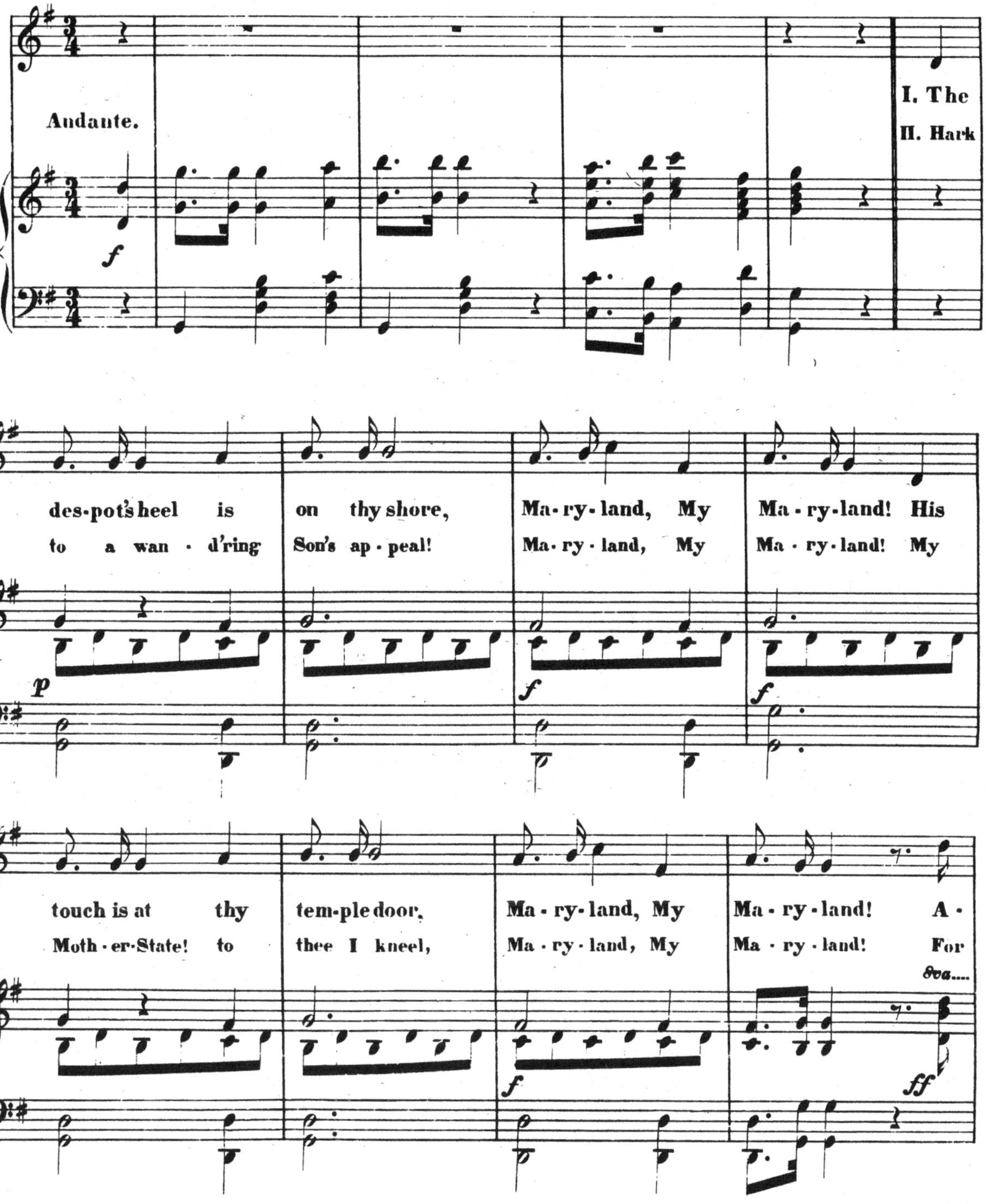

II. Hark to a wan-d'ring Son's ap-peal! Ma-ry-land, My Ma-ry-land! My Moth-er-State! to thee I kneel, Ma-ry-land, My Ma-ry-land! For

f p f f f ff 8va....

-venge the pa - tri - ot - ic gore That fleck'd the streets of Bal - ti - more, And
life and death, for woe and weal, Thy peer - less chiv - al - ry re - veal, And
8va
be the Bat - tle - Queen of yore, Ma - ry - land, My Ma - ry - land!
gird thy beau - teous limbs with steel, Ma - ry - land, My Ma - ry - land!
p
8va
ff

3

Thou wilt not cower in the dust,
Maryland! My Maryland!
Thy beaming sword shall never rust,
Maryland! My Maryland!
Remember Carroll's sacred trust,
Remember Howard's warlike thrust—
And all thy slumberers with the just,
Maryland! My Maryland!

4

Come! for thy shield is bright and strong,
Maryland! My Maryland!
Come! for thy dalliance, does thee wrong,
Maryland! My Maryland!
Come! to thine own heroic throng,
That stalks with Liberty along,
And give a new Key to thy song,
Maryland! My Maryland!

5

Dear Mother! burst the tyrant's chain,
Maryland! My Maryland!
Virginia should not call in vain!
Maryland! My Maryland!
She meets her sisters on the plain—
"Sic semper" tis the proud refrain,
That baffles minions back amain,
Maryland! My Maryland!

6

I see the blush upon thy cheek,
Maryland! My Maryland!
But thou wast ever bravely meek,
Maryland! My Maryland!
But lo! there surges forth a shriek
From hill to hill, from creek to creek—
Potomac calls to Chesapeake,
Maryland! My Maryland!

7

Thou wilt not yield the vandal toll,
Maryland! My Maryland!
Thou wilt not crook to his control,
Maryland! My Maryland!
Better the fire upon thee roll,
Better the blade, the shot, the bowl,
Than crucifixion of the soul,
Maryland! My Maryland!

8

I hear the distant thunder-hum,
Maryland! My Maryland!
The Old Line's bugle, fife and drum,
Maryland! My Maryland!
She is not dead, nor deaf, nor dumb—
Huzza! she spurns the Northern scum!
She breathes— she burns! she'll come! she'll come!
Maryland! My Maryland!

Massachusetts

"All Hail to Massachusetts"

"All Hail to Massachusetts" was adopted as the official State Song of Massachusetts by Chapter 383 of the Acts of 1981. The song was written by Arthur J. Marsh Sr.

In 1966, Chapter 644 of the Acts of 1966 established "All Hail to Massachusetts" as the song of the commonwealth. The song was selected from approximately 80 submissions to a commission, headed by the conductor Arthur Fiedler, that existed from 1958 to 1965.

History compiled by Hladczuk and Hladczuk.

ALL HAIL TO MASSACHUSETTS

PATRIOTIC SONG

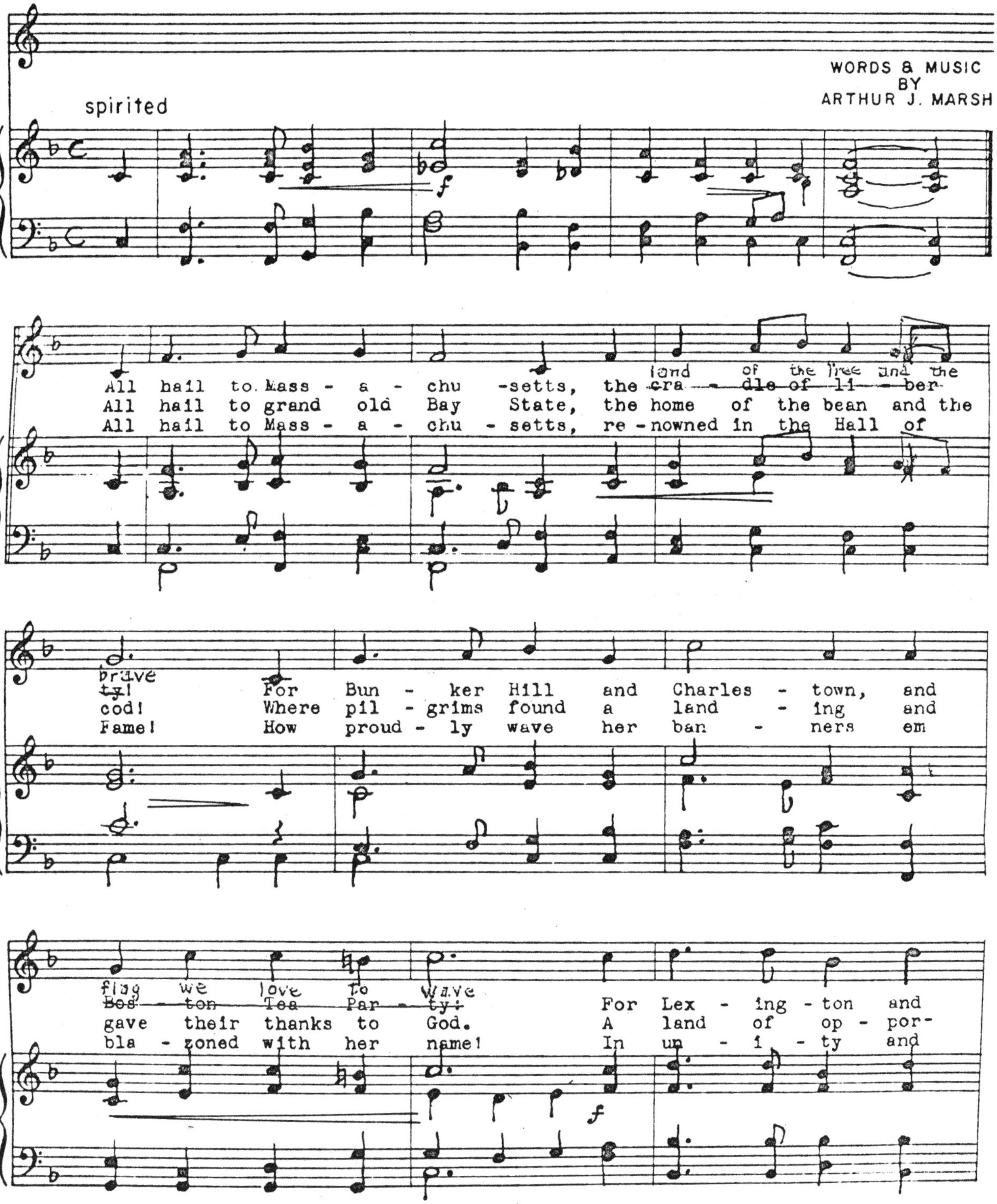
WORDS & MUSIC BY ARTHUR J. MARSH
spirited
land of the free and the
All hail to Mass - a - chu -setts, the cra - dle of li - ber
All hail to grand old Bay State, the home of the bean and the
All hail to Mass - a - chu - setts, re - nowned in the Hall of
brave
ty! For Bun - ker Hill and Charles - town, and
cod! Where pil - grims found a land - ing and
Fame! How proud - ly wave her ban - ners em
flag we love to wave
Bos - ton Tea Par - ty: For Lex - ing - ton and
gave their thanks to God. A land of op - por-
bla - zoned with her name! In un - i - ty and

COPYRIGHT 1954 A. J. MARSH

Con - - cord, and the shot heard 'round the world: All
tu - ni - ty in the good old U. S. A. Where
bro - ther - hood, sons and daugh - ters go hand in hand: All
hail to Mass- a - chu - setts, we'll keep her flag un - furled. She
men live long and pros - per, and peo -ple come to stay. Don't
hail to Mass - a - chu - setts, there is no fi - ner land! It's
stands up-right for free -dom's light that shines from sea to sea: All
sell her short but learn to court her in - dus - try and stride: All
M - A - S - S - A - C - H - U - S - E - T - T - S. All
hail to Mass - a - chu - setts! Our coun - try 'tis of thee!
hail to grand old Bay State! The land of pil - grim's pride!
hail to Mass - a - chu - setts! All hail! All hail! All hail!
f
r - i - t - a - r - d.

Minnesota

"Hail! Minnesota"

The Minnesota state song, "Hail! Minnesota," was adopted as the official state song in 1945. The music and first verse were written by Truman E. Rickard as part of a senior class play at the University of Minnesota. It was subsequently adopted as the University of Minnesota song. When the song was adopted by the state legislature, the phrase "Hail to thee our state so dear" took the place of the original phrase, "Hail to thee our college dear."

Truman E. Rickard was born in Minneapolis on January 22, 1882. He graduated from the University of Minnesota in 1904. Mr. Rickard also wrote the Minnesota fight song, "Minnesota Let's Go!" He died on April 18, 1948, in Fosston, Minnesota.

The second verse of "Hail! Minnesota" was written by Arthur E. Upson. Mr. Upson, a poet, was born in Camden, New Jersey, on January 10, 1877. He graduated from the University of Minnesota in 1905, and lived in the Minneapolis/St. Paul area while pursuing his literary career. He died on August 14, 1908.

History compiled by Hladczuk and Hladczuk.

Hail! Minnesota

Mississippi

"Go, Mississippi"

Helped by an advisory committee, the Jackson Board of Realtors sought and selected "Go, Mississippi" by Houston Davis as the song that would best serve the interests of the State of Mississippi and all Mississippians. In 1962, the song was made the official state song by House Concurrent Resolution Number 67, adopted by the House of Representatives and the Senate. The resolution specified that "the Mississippi Agricultural and Industrial Board, all other agencies of the State, and all persons, firms, or organizations interested in promoting the welfare of the state of Mississippi are specifically authorized and empowered, in accordance with the law, to make use of the state song, 'Go Mississippi,' in promoting and advancing the cause of the State of Mississippi and its citizens."

Thus "Go Mississippi" joined the ranks of officially adopted works, including a poem titled "Mississippi," which was adopted as the "State Ode" in March 1902. Prior to 1962, there had been two official state songs, each replaced by the next official state song. The first, adopted in 1917 by Dunbar Rowland, the director of the Mississippi Department of Archives and History was Mrs. Dunbar Rowland's "Mississippi," set to music by Walter Aiken and published as the state song in the biennial reports of the Secretary of State. The second was "Way Down South in Mississippi," which the legislature adopted with Senate Concurrent Resolution Number 36 in 1948 until 1962, when the legislature stated that the "present official song had served its purpose" but was no longer representative of the "quickening pace of development of the State of Mississippi."

The words and music of the present song were written by Houston Davis, who also held the copyright to the song. However, a newspaper article by Charles B. Gordon, a *Daily News* staff writer, noted that the copyright was assigned to the Jackson Board of Realtors in 1962.

History compiled by Sharon S. Hladczuk.

2

GO, MISSISSIPPI

Mississippi Official State Song–Adopted by Legislature 1962, May 16

4.

GO MISSISSIPPI, continue to roll,
Grow Mississippi the top is the goal
GO MISSISSIPPI, you'll have and you'll hold
M-I-S-S-I-S-S-I-P-P-I.

5.

GO MISSISSIPPI, get up and go,
GO MISSISSIPPI, let the world know
That our Mississippi is leading the show,
M-I-S-S-I-S-S-I-P-P-I.

Go Mississippi - 2

Missouri

"The Missouri Waltz"

"The Missouri Waltz" has at last come into its own and been declared the state song of Missouri. Passed by both houses of the 65th General Assembly, the bill naming it as the official song was signed by Governor Forrest Smith, June 30, 1949.

There has been a great deal of mystery connected with the origin of the old familiar waltz, and various stories have appeared from time to time purporting to carry the true facts of its inception. After Harry S. Truman became President of the United States and it was discovered that the "Missouri Waltz" was his favorite song, the stories appeared with increasing regularity. Most of the versions agree on the fact that the song was first arranged and published by Frederic Knight Logan, a noted musician of Oskaloosa, Iowa, who had picked it up from John Valentine Eppel, an orchestra leader of Fort Dodge, Iowa. According to one version of the story appearing in the St. Louis *Globe-Democrat* of October 21, 1945, which was reviewed in the *Missouri Historical Review* XL (April 1946), 443–444, Eppel learned the melody from a Missouri Negro who in turn had been taught the tune by his mother. Around Moberly, citizens insist that the original composer was Dab Hannah, a Negro piano player, but in Oskaloosa some say that Henry Clay Cooper, a Negro dancing teacher, gave the melody to Logan.

Another story concerning the "Missouri Waltz" comes from an article by Chester A. Bradley in the *Kansas City Star* of March 29, 1949, and reprinted in the July 1949 issue of the *Missouri Historical Review.* According to Bradley, the late Edgar Lee Settle of New Franklin, a gifted piano player who traveled with musical shows, obtained the tune from the DiArmo sisters, a musical team on his theatrical circuit, who in turn had been given it "by an old darkey down South." J. Boulton Settle, Edgar's brother and editor of the *New Franklin News,* insists that Edgar composed the piece, which he called the "Graveyard Waltz." According to Bill Corum of the *New York Journal,* who is quoted by Bradley in his article, Edgar was playing it in Moberly one evening when John Eppel heard it and used it with his orchestra from then on.

The story of the song is well-known after Frederic Knight Logan received it. In 1914, the Forster Publishing Company of Chicago secured the rights to the melody from Logan and with lyrics composed by Jim Shannon, it appeared in 1916 as the "Hush-a-Bye Ma Baby" song, with "Missouri Waltz" printed as a subtitle in parentheses. It soon swept the country and became the second most popular sheet-music seller from the day of its publication [1949].

History courtesy of the
Missouri Historical Review (October 1949),
vol. 44, number 1, pages 71–72.

★ If necessary, the lowest note in right hand chords and octaves, may be omitted.

Visit Your Record Store For Recordings Of "Missouri Waltz"

4
Dm
Strum, strum, strum, strum, strum,
Cm
Seems I
hear those ban-jos
A7
play - in' once a -
Dm
gain, Hum, hum,
hum, hum, hum, That same old
A7
plain - tive
Dm
strain.
pf
p
Interlude
f
p
Hush 5

5
Dm A7 Dm A7 Dm
Hear that mourn - ful mel - o - dy, It just haunts you the
mp
A7 Dm B♭ F
whole day long, And you wan-der in dreams back to Dix-ie, it
f ff fff L.H. pp
G7 C7 F
seems, When you hear that old - time song.
pp
1st Mo.
F C7 F
Hush - a-bye, ma ba - by, go to sleep on Mom-my's knee, Jour - ney back to
p
Hush 5

6
C7 F Bb
Dix - ie - land in dreams a - gain with me; It seems like your Mom - my is
F G7 C7
there once a - gain, And the old folks were strum - min' that same old re - frain.
F C7 F
'Way down in Mis - sou - ri where I learned this lul - la - by, When the stars were
C7 F Bb Dm
blink - in' and the moon was climb - in' high, Seems I hear voic - es low, as in
F G7 C7 F
days long a - go Sing - in' hush - a - bye.
rit.
Hush 5

Montana

"Montana"

The music and lyrics of "Montana" were written as the result of an evening dinner-party challenge put to Joseph E. Howard (music) and Charles Cohan (lyrics). From that half-hour genesis sprang the body of what would eventually become the Montana state song; the remainder of "Montana" was written that same evening.

"Montana" was first sung in the presence of Governor Edwin L. Norris. The song received 12 curtain calls. The next day, when Governor Norris met with Howard and Cohan, the governor wanted to approve the song as the state song, but Howard and Cohan wanted to donate the song to a worthy charity. "Montana" was eventually donated to the Montana Children's Home, in Helena.

Joseph Howard went on to write musical comedies and songs. Some of his more popular songs were "What's the Use of Dreaming," "Shuffle off to Buffalo," and "I Wonder Who's Kissing Her Now."

Charles Cohan became a newspaperman who also wrote the Montana-based novel entitled *Born of the Crucible.*

"Montana" became the official state song of Montana on February 20, 1945.

History compiled by Hladczuk and Hladczuk.

OFFICIAL STATE SONG *adopted by* GOV. EDWIN L. NORRIS, 1910

"Montana."

Montana - 3 Music by Jos. E. Howard, composer of "I Wonder Who's Kissing Her Now" and several hundred other popular songs.
Lyrics by Chas. C Cohan, Author of "My Treasure State"

4
REFRAIN
Mon - ta - na, Mon - ta - na, Glo-ry of the West ___ Of
p-f
all the states from coast to coast. You're eas - i - ly the best ___ Mon -
ta - na, Mon - ta - na, Where skies are al-ways blue M - O -
N - T - A - N - A, Mon-ta-na, I love you. ___ Mon - you. ___
1
2
Montana - 3
RAYNER, DALHEIM & CO. MUSIC PRINTERS CHICAGO

Nebraska

"Beautiful Nebraska"

The Jim Fras story and how he came to Nebraska to write its official song begins in the Soviet Union where Jim was born.

His interest in music began at age 6. Jim was in that part of Russia occupied by the German Army in World War II. His father had died before the war. When the Germans came, they shipped his mother and two sisters to a labor camp in Germany.

When the Nazis moved out, Mr. Fras followed into Germany. When he reached the labor camp, he discovered that his mother and the sisters had returned to Russia. He decided to stay, along with a number of other displaced persons.

In Germany, he met and married Irene Horak. They lived in a refugee camp. In the camp, Jim ate poisonous food. The after-effects left him paralyzed. "I was hopeless," he said, "until an ex-German Army orthopedic physician took my case. He decided to use the piano as my therapy."

The physician became rough when Jim complained that it was "impossible" for him to play. "One day, he locked me in a room with a piano, placed me on a bench next to the instrument and told me to hit C-minor," he said. "I said it was impossible."

Jim cried, crawled across the floor and knocked on the door with his cane. The doctor refused to listen. Finally, after two hours, Jim managed to get back to the piano. "Somehow I spread my hand so that I hit C-minor."

That's when the doctor came back into the room. Jim called him a "Nazi swine," but the doctor insisted, "we're going to have you playing again in no time."

Recovery has not been complete, but Jim can walk without a cane. His trip to the United States with wife and two sons came indirectly as the result of his "falling for the Americans while I played for them in a club."

He came to Lincoln in 1952. He has had a variety of jobs, ranging from janitor for a candy company to having his own radio variety show.

"Beautiful Nebraska" was created after Jim took a ride in the country. He noted the wave of the wheat fields, saw the green valleys and "loved everything I saw."

The music was written entirely by Mr. Fras. Guy G. Miller, a Lincoln friend, helped with the words, which Jim says "are about 85 percent mine."

This was the writer's second attempt to have his selection accepted by the Legislature. In 1963, Jim was unable even to get a committee to "listen to my music."

Two years later, the Centennial Commission indicated it would take over the project. The official song ran into more controversy within the commission.

It was probably academic when the Legislature finally selected Jim's song in the spring of 1968. Before it acted, many schools were already singing the words.

Jim received a letter from a friend the other day, which the song writer says best expresses his feelings.

It stated: "Remember that while a Legislature can make a song official, it's only the people who can make it their song."

Story by James Denney, *Sunday Magazine of the Midlands, Omaha World-Herald,* Omaha, Nebraska, August 28, 1968.

Beautiful Nebraska

The Official Nebraska State Song

Words by JIM FRAS
and GUY G. MILLER

Music by JIM FRAS

W. M. Co. 9547

gm
C7
Dm
A7
as you look a - round, You will find a rain - bow rea - ching to the ground;
B♭
B♭m
F
A7
Dm
gm
C7
F
All these won - ders by the Mas - ter's hand; Beau - ti - ful Ne - bra - ska land.
F7
F7
or Aaug. Faug.
B♭
B♭
We are so proud of this state where we live,

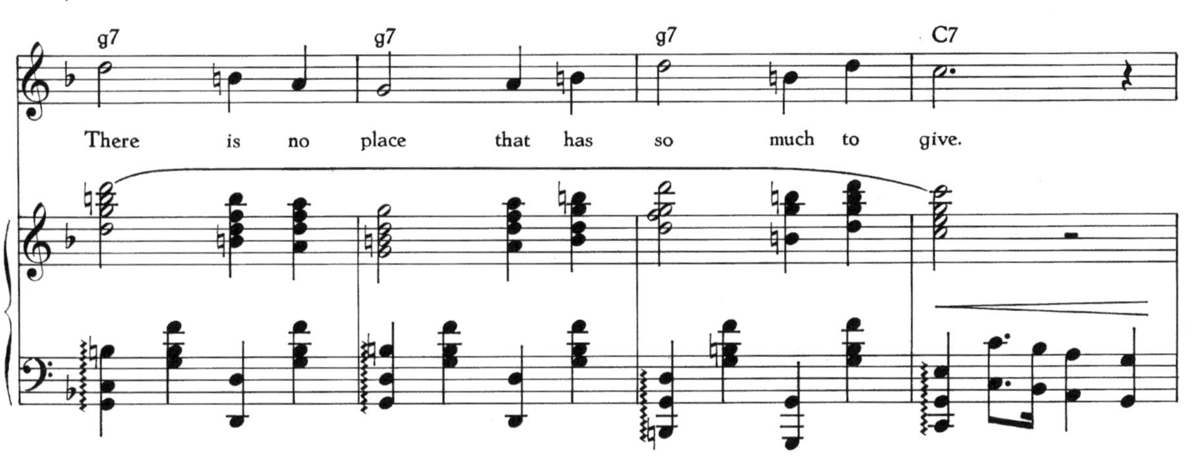
g7
g7
g7
C7
There is no place that has so much to give.

fF
Cdim.
gm
C7
Dm
A7
Beau-ti-ful Ne-bra-ska, as you look a-round, you will find a rain-bow rea-ching to the ground:
f

B♭
B♭m
F
A7
Dm
gm
C7
F
All these won-ders by the Mas-ter's hand. Beau-ti-ful Ne-bra-ska land.

W. M. Co. 9547

Nevada

"Home Means Nevada"

In the summer of 1932, Nevada Native Daughters invited me to sing a Nevada Song of my choice at their annual picnic at Bowers Mansion in August of that year. I accepted that invitation with considerable pleasure.

While I found many lovely Nevada songs, none of them expressed *my* admiration, esteem, and affection for Nevada. Then I recalled that several years prior, I had written a song of Nevada. That manuscript had been laid aside because it did not fulfill the demands of my deep desire to express, musically and lyrically, my truest emotions for the Battle Born State—Nevada.

I wanted to express in a simple, natural style those enduring and homely qualities I had found in Nevada—the same qualities one finds in a good home . . . beauty, joy, and security. During the lapse of time between my first notes of this song and the year of 1932, I had made considerable progress in my musical and lyrical studies, and felt I could, now, revise that manuscript to my satisfaction. I set about the work with renewed interest.

However, I had scarcely assembled my old notes, when unexpected . . . and very welcome . . . house guests arrived. In haste, I marked my calendar (an error of one week too late . . . for the promised performance!). Two weeks of fun passed by, and on the morning my guests were leaving, I read with consternation . . . that the Native Daughters' picnic was to be celebrated the next day—and not one note of that song I had promised to sing had been written!

Before ten o'clock that Saturday morning, I flew to the piano before my friend's automobile had turned the corner. I did not wonder if I could write that song. I was sure that I could; was sure of my technique; sure of precisely what I wanted to express. It really isn't difficult to say "I love you" to an adored one whom you have known and loved for a long, long time . . . so long that your heart is very close to your lips.

From ten a.m. that Saturday, until four a.m. the next morning, I wrote without stopping. Then happy and satisfied, I laid aside the first verse and chorus of my song and retired. That same afternoon, I sang and played from a lead-pencil script, "Home Means Nevada"—on the front balcony of Bowers Mansion.

The song was so beautifully received that my heart still glows with gratitude for that Nevada-loving audience. As I arose from the piano, a very distinguished-looking elderly gentleman slowly rose [sic] up from where he was sitting behind me, and barred my exit from the platform. He propped his gold-headed ebony cane against the old square piano; removed his high topper from his leonine head, looking every inch the statesman, and said to me, "Honey, that's the prettiest Nevada song that I have ever heard. It should be made the State Song of Nevada!" Then, he placed his trembling hands upon my shoulders and kissed me . . . one cheek and the other.

That gentleman was the Honorable Roswell K. Colcord, a Great Governor of the Great State of Nevada, 1891–1894. A few moments later, the Honorable Morley Griswold, Lieutenant Governor, 1925–1935, and Acting Governor, 1934–1935, of Nevada, echoed the sentiments expressed by Ex-Governor Colcord. Many more similar expressions from those present followed in swift succession.

There is the true story of why, when, and how I wrote "Home Means Nevada." The rest is history and may be found in the Statutes of

Nevada, 1933, under the caption of Senate Bill No. 7 (adopted February 6, 1933).

Other facts regarding this song, I believe, should be made of record and known at this time. I append a few such facts:

While I was and am convinced that I wrote a song that was both musically and lyrically sound; that it was very singable; and that it appealed to as many as had heard it, there remained a majority of Nevada's citizens who had had little opportunity to hear and judge that song before it went to the Legislature. With limited means, I did all I could to supply that deficit. I sang that song whenever requested—an actual count of 187 times in three months! Finally, the song went to the Nevada Legislature, accompanied by an imposing file of endorsements from people in all walks of life—even an extra letter from Al Greenbaum, Secretary of the National Musicians Union, he being at the time a resident of Nevada. How proud I was to sing for both Houses of Legislature, and how deeply I was moved by the honors accorded me before they adopted unanimously "Home Means Nevada," as the Official State Song!

Because of a widely prevalent and absolutely erroneous impression that must still be in the public mind—it pops up so frequently!—I wish to dispel forever the implication that I have ever received any compensation from the State of Nevada for the song; it should be remembered that the world was in the throes of a depression in 1932–1933, and Nevada was no exception.

I did not request payment for this song, nor did I receive any—other than the personal satisfaction that accrues from the contribution to cultural progress. How abhorrent it would have been to me, to ask for money for a song when so many were needing bread!

History by Mrs. Bertha Raffetto
and used by permission of the
Nevada State Library & Archives.

NEVADA STATE SONG.
By Act of LEGISLATURE Feb. 6. 1933.

Tune Ukulele
G C E A

Home Means Nevada

Home Means Nevada - 3

5
Dmin
G7
C
sil - ver - y rills, Out where the sun al - ways shines,
Gdim
G7
C
G7
C7
There is the land that I love the best, Fair - er than all I can
F
Cdim
C
F
C
G7
see. Right in the heart of the gold - en west
C
G7
1 C
G7
C
G7
2 C
F
C
Home, means Ne - va - da to me. me.
Home Means Nevada - 3

New Hampshire

"Old New Hampshire"

New Hampshire has the unusual distinction of having eight state songs, with one of them being "official" and others "honorary." This came about by legislative votes over a quarter of a century, and was finally agreed upon in the 1977 session.

Back in 1949, the Legislature adopted "Old New Hampshire" as the official state song. It was written in 1926, with the music by Maurice Hoffmann Jr., organist of the Franklin Street Congregational church in Manchester, and the words by Dr. John F. Holmes of that city. The 1941 Legislature turned down this song, and the 1943 Legislature killed a bill proposed by Rep. Samuel P. Philbrook of Belmont for a $1,500 public contest to pick a state song, with a $500 prize for the music and $300 for the words, along with $700 for a team of judges and related expenses.

The 1963 Legislature approved a "Second State Song." It was "New Hampshire, My New Hampshire," by Julius Richelson and Walter P. Smith of Plymouth. Then the 1973 Legislature added a "Third State Song." It was "New Hampshire Hills," with the music by Tom Powers of Detroit, Michigan, son of retired Director Edward Powers of the State Sweepstakes Commission, and the late Paul S. Maurer, state poet laureate.

The 1977 Legislature voted in two unusual song laws. Early in March, it adopted a "Fourth State Song." It was "Autumn In New Hampshire," by Leo Austin of Warner. At the same time, the legislators created an interim board to recommend one official state song, with the label "honorary" for each of the others.

Rep. Richardson D. Benton of Chester, chairman of the House Committee on Public Protection and Veterans Affairs, became coordinator of a State Song Selection Board. Appointed by the Governor and Council were William E. Elwell of Portsmouth, who became chairman, and Ted Hebert and Robert F. Thibault of Manchester, along with Senator Robert F. Bossie of Manchester, named by the Senate President, and Rep. Jane F. Sanders of Alton Bay, named by the House Speaker.

Three months after this Board was launched, the Legislature enacted another song law, effective June 15. This statute added four more songs to the listing of state songs, with a proviso that if the Board did not designate any of this quartet as the official state song, they would become "honorary." The Board heard and considered a total of 21 songs, all submitted by New Hampshire residents.

Announcement of the name of the official song was made in Representatives Hall on November 29, 1977, when Mrs. Gale Thomson, wife of Governor Meldrim Thomson, Jr., drew the choice from a sealed envelope in which the name had been placed by the Board.

The four additional state songs were "New Hampshire's Granite State" by Annie B. Currier of Londonderry; "Oh, New Hampshire (You're My Home)" by Brownie McIntosh of

Hampton; "The Old Man of the Mountain" by Paul Belanger of Berlin; and "The New Hampshire State March" by Rene Richards of Nashua.

Coordinator Benton officially reported that the Board had voted to give the exclusive title of the official state song to the original state song of "Old New Hampshire," and this action is officially recorded as a footnote to the law creating eight state songs, in New Hampshire's Revised Statutes Annotated.

History courtesy of the State of New Hampshire, Department of State, Division of Records Management and Archives. Source: *State of New Hampshire: Manual for the General Court*, No. 47 (1981) (Concord: Secretary of State, 1981).

OLD NEW HAMPSHIRE

lakes, the fields, the for-ests; Made the riv-ers and the rills; Made the
maj-es-ty of moun-tain; Hers, the grand-eur of the lake; Hers, the
bub-bling, crys-tal foun-tains Of New Hampshire's Gran-ite Hills.
truth as from the hill-side Whence her crys-tal wat-ers break.
REFRAIN
Old New Hampshire, Old New Hamp-shire, Old New Hamp-shire, grand and great, We will
sing of Old New Hamp-shire, Of the dear old Gran-ite State.
D. S. 𝄋
D. S. 𝄋

New Mexico

"O, Fair New Mexico"

"O, Fair New Mexico" was written in 1914 by Elizabeth Garrett, who was the blind daughter of Sheriff Pat Garrett. You may remember Sheriff Garrett as the person who in July 1881 shot and killed the outlaw Billy the Kid in a house near Fort Sumner, New Mexico.

"O, Fair New Mexico" was adopted as the official state song in 1916.

Miss Garrett had stated that the song was not written "for market" but rather was inspired by her love for New Mexico.

History compiled by Hladczuk and Hladczuk.

"Así Es Nuevo México"

Amadeo Lucero was born in Rinconada, New Mexico, April 1, 1900. He had two brothers and one sister. He married at age 28 to Frances Miera, who died in 1949; they had ten children (eight survived).

He attended Menaul School—a Presbyterian school for boys—in Albuquerque, New Mexico, and graduated in the class of 1923. He was involved with the music program and played the trumpet and saxophone. He also played football. He attended the University of New Mexico and Highlands University in Las Vegas, New Mexico.

After high school he had a band called the Blue Birds, and they played to enthusiastic crowds in northern New Mexico.

He was an elementary school teacher for 36 years and was loved by his students, who maintained contact with him after many years, often stopping him on the street to reminisce. He was well known, admired, and respected throughout the northern part of New Mexico.

Amadeo frequently visited elementary schools encouraging students to apply themselves in school and become upstanding citizens. He also encouraged Hispanics to be proud of their heritage and to be actively involved in the American mainstream.

"Así Es Nuevo México" was adopted as an official state song in 1971.

Mr. Lucero passed on in Albuquerque on August 20, 1987.

History compiled by Amadeo Lucero's children with additions by Hladczuk and Hladczuk.

litation

Santa Fe, N. Mex.
Marzo 1971.
escribió
Antonio Mendoza G.

FIRST VERSE

UN CANTO QUE TRAIGO MUY DENTRO DEL ALMA
LO CANTO A MI ESTADO - MI TIERRA NATAL,
DE FLORES DORADA MI TIERRA ENCANTADA
DE LINDAS MUJERES - QUE NO TIENE IGUAL.

CHORUS

ASI ES NUEVO MEJICO
ASI ES ESTA TIERRA DEL SOL
DE SIERRAS Y VALLES DE TIERRAS FRUTALES
ASI ES NUEVO MEJICO

SECOND VERSE

EL NEGRO, EL HISPANO, EL ANGLO, EL INDIO
TODOS SON TUS HIJOS, TODOS POR IGUAL.
TUS PUEBLOS Y ALDEAS - MI TIERRA ENCANTADA
DE LINDAS MUJERES QUE NO TIENE IGUAL.

(CHORUS)

THIRD VERSE

EL RIO DEL NORTE, QUE ES EL RIO GRANDE,
SUS AGUAS CORRIENTES FLUYEN HASTA EL MAR
Y RIEGAN LOS CAMPOS
MI TIERRA ENCANTADA DE LINDAS MUJERES
QUE NO TIENE IGUAL.

(CHORUS)

FOURTH VERSE

TUS CAMPOS SE VISTEN DE FLORES DE MAYO
DE LINDOS COLORES
QUE DIOS LES DOTÓ
TUS PAJAROS CANTAN MI TIERRA ENCANTADA
SUS TRINOS DE AMORES
AL SER CELESTIAL.

(CHORUS)

FIFTH VERSE

MI TIERRA ENCANTADA DE HISTORIA BAÑADA
TAN LINDA, TAN BELLA - SIN COMPARACIÓN.
TE RINDO HOMENAJE, TE RINDO CARIÑO
SOLDADO VALIENTE - TE RINDE SU AMOR.

(CHORUS)

Official State Song

O, Fair New Mexico

Words & Music
BY ELIZABETH GARRETT

*) Mejico-pronounced: Mĕ-hĭ-cō.

687-3-1

4
Home of the Mon - te - zu - ma, With fiery heart a - glow,
Fields full of sweet al - fal - fa, Rich - est perfumes be - stow,
Land with its bright mañ - a - na, Com - ing through weal and woe,
State of the deeds his - tor - ic, Is Nue - vo Me - ji - co.
State of the ap - ple blossoms, Is Nue - vo Me - ji - co.
State of our es - per - an - za, Is Nue - vo Me - ji - co.
rit.
rit.
REFRAIN
Slightly faster
O, fair New Mex - i - co, We love, we love you so,
f
mf
a tempo
Con 8va
687-3-2

Our hearts with pride o'er - flow
No mat - ter where we go,
O, fair New
Mex - i - co,
We love, we love you so,
The grand-est state to know,
New Mex-i - co.
co.
mf a tempo
Ped * Ped *
1 2
f accelerando
Con 8va
D.S. 3
a tempo
accelerando
Con 8va
Con 8va

New York

"I Love New York"

There is a touching story behind Gov. Hugh L. Carey's proclamation of "I Love New York" as the state's theme song.

Steve Karmen, the son of an immigrant, is the author of the words and music. Many may not know he is the same man who wrote such well-known jingles for the advertising world as "Weekends Were Made for Michelob," and "When You Say Budweiser, You've Said It All." Altogether he has won 14 Clio awards—the advertising world's equivalent of Oscars—and he has written about 2,000 other advertising jingles during his career.

Anyway, when he showed up in Albany . . . to be honored by Carey for writing "I Love New York," he displayed a touch of humility not usually associated with people from the Big Apple. First of all, he gave the state the right, in perpetuity, to use "I Love New York" as the state song. So that eliminates the profit motive.

Finally, after giving all the proper credits to associates and friends for their collaboration, Steve asked, and received, permission to dedicate the song to a special person. Here's how he handled it:

> In 1912, a young boy emigrated to America from his birthplace in Russia. He was 13 years old, the eldest son of 12 children. He learned how to speak English, went to school, later got a job, went to college at night and received a degree in engineering, and became crippled, and many of the major decisions of family life were left to the eldest son. When others emigrated to America from the family, some chose to settle farther west. Not only did he choose to remain in New York and to live in New York and to marry in New York and to raise his children in New York, but when it came time to pick his career direction, he went to work for the City of New York. And, when he retired in 1969, he had been a Civil Service employee for 44 years.
>
> If my father were here today, he would be the proudest of all of us. Proud not only for his son's achievement, but proud for yet another confirmation of the miracle that is America—where the son of an immigrant could stand with the Governor of the state and be honored as the composer of the state song.
>
> And, so in memory of Hyman Karmen, I dedicate "I Love New York" to the people of New York State, with the hope that every time it is heard, it will be a reminder to residents and visitors of a way of life and style that is unequaled anywhere. Thank you, very much.

The room was filled with presumably heartless politicians, inconsiderate state officials, and hard-nosed newsmen when Steve Karmen spoke, but it was quiet. You could hear a pin drop.

And for some strange reason, when he finished there was a rustling all through the room, and seldom-used handkerchiefs appeared, and there was a chorus of nose-blowing and eye-dabbing.

Public officials, politicians, newspaper reporters, and, yes everyone need to hear a story like that every once in awhile to remember that America is indeed a miracle for many; it is still the land of opportunity, and it's the best darned country in the world. It needs more people like Steve Karmen to remind us.

History source: This brief history first appeared in the *Syracuse Post-Standard* in an editorial written by Fred Fiske.

I LOVE NEW YORK
The Official Theme Of New York

Words and Music by
STEVE KARMEN

PV1216/1-5

Dm/A
Em
Em/B
you go, and no - bod - y can com - pare it,
F
F/C
Cmaj9
it's win and place and show, you know. New York is spe -
C7/E
C9
Fmaj7
D7/F♯
cial, you know. New York is diff - 'rent 'cause there's
C/G
Am7
Dm
no place else on earth quite like New York.

PV1216/2-5

G
to Coda
Cmaj9
C6/G
Cmaj9
And that's why
I
love
New
Dm9
F
G
Cmaj9
York.
'cause it's so
ex - cit - ing.
I
C6/G
Cmaj9
Dm9
F
G
love
New
York.
and there's no
place
like
it.
Play 3 times

PV1216/3-5

F
C/G
G
I love New York.
F/G
C/G
G
I love New York.
F/G
G
I love New York.
F
F/G
G
I love New York.

PV1216/4-5

F
G
D.S. al Coda
Coda
Cmaj9
C6/G
Dm9
I love New York. 'cause it's so ex - cit - ing.
I love New York. and there's no place like it.
Repeat and fade

PV1216/5-5

North Carolina

"The Old North State"

From about the year 1835, over a century ago, the people of North Carolina loyally sang as their state song "The Old North State," but it was not until 1927, by an act of the State Legislature, that it became the official state song.

The little office in Raleigh where Judge Gaston wrote the words of "The Old North State" stood on the corner of Hargett and Salisbury Streets. A bronze tablet commemorating this fact was placed there in 1928 by the Caswell-Nash Chapter of the Daughters of the American Revolution.

Two traditional stories have come down to us concerning the origin of the music of "The Old North State." In one story, perhaps not so well known, it is related that Judge Gaston, while attending an opera in New York City, in company with a lady (who evidently did not think North Carolina was a very interesting state in which to live), heard a tune he liked so well that he said to his companion: "If you will send me the music to that waltz, I will write a poem on North Carolina that will cause you to change your opinion of my state."

This story, however, does not have quite as much to support it as the other one, which has been generally told and accepted throughout the years. It is as follows:

A group of "Swiss Bell-Ringers" at a program given in Raleigh in 1835 sang a song that appealed to several North Carolina girls, who hummed it over and over on the way home. The next day two of them "begged a copy of the music from the leader of the company" and that night sang the melody under the window of Judge Gaston's residence. According to tradition, Judge Gaston was so pleased with the serenade that he said: "But there should be some words to such a pretty tune." Judge Gaston at this time was living in the home of Mrs. James F. Taylor, which was located at 102–104 West Hargett Street, Raleigh. One evening while Miss Louisa Taylor, a little girl of 13, was playing the air on the piano, her mother remarked to Judge Gaston: "Uncle, what an appropriate tune for a national hymn." Soon afterwards William Gaston wrote words for this tune which had been sung by the "Swiss Bell-Ringers."

Thus the music of "The Old North State" came to us at a period in the history of our country when immigration was at its height. In this way America had brought to her shores much of the folk music of the whole world.

A comparison of the few printings of the music of "The Old North State" reveals the fact that the state song of North Carolina has gone through a series of transformations like that of the folk song. The folk element is evident in the variations that have appeared in the way it has been sung in different periods of the lifetime of older people now living in different sections of the state. Variations in this song have occurred in different localities because of the fact that the song has been perpetuated largely by oral transmission.

There are three articles of historical interest which give touches of local color to the writing of the words of "The Old North State"—each one giving a slightly different account. Perrin Busbee in the *North Carolina University Magazine*, March–April 1894, tells about the old Taylor home in Raleigh where Judge Gaston lived and the law office on the same lot where he wrote the words of "The Old North State."

Jacques Busbee, writing in the *North Carolina Booklet*, April 1913, tells of the interest his great-grandmother's family, the Taylors, had in this song of the Tyrolean singers and how they cooperated with Judge Gaston in order to get the meter to fit the song. His story is an account of a personal conversation he had with his great-aunt, Miss Louisa Taylor, concerning the writing of the words of "The Old North State."

Col. Fred A. Olds, in an article preserved in the Hall of History, relates how he secured for the Historical Commission the original manuscript of this folk song from Mrs. Malinda B. Ray, Fayetteville, "who for over 40 years had kept as one of her most treasured possessions this sheet of written music with its German words, handsomely written." Col. Olds also quotes a memorandum about "The Old North State" given him by Capt. S. A. Ashe, the historian of Raleigh: "Several little girls, among them Louisa Taylor, Fannie Birdsall, and Lossie Hill, heard the concert by the Tyrolean singers and went home singing the air."

Strange as it may seem, the writer was able to locate only four printings of "The Old North State" prior to 1926: the first is to be found in *Wiley's North Carolina Reader*, published in 1851 by James M. Edney, Asheville, North Carolina; the second was published by Alfred Williams and Company, Raleigh, sometime between the years 1893 and 1900 (a copy of this printing is in the State Library); the third appeared in "Songs of the Seasons," a collection of songs published in 1909 by Mary Best Jones of New Bern and is "harmonized by Francis X. Hale"; the fourth is in a handbill form printed by the Rotary Club of Washington, North Carolina, for distribution to all Rotary Clubs in the state. This arrangement is by the late Edmund H. Harding of Washington, North Carolina, who said: "I made the arrangements in accordance with the way I had been taught as a child to sing the song."

The writer found in different sections of the state that, like a folk song, the people transmitted "The Old North State" orally from one generation to the next; that in the main, the body of the song was more or less the same, with extra quarter or eighth notes added here and there or slight changes in the melody.

Ever since the days of the Francis X. Hale harmonization, younger generations have been singing "The Old North State" in their bright, happy way with a quick, rousing "Hurrah." They have added here and there dotted notes in the body of the tune.

Following the legislative enactment of 1927, when the words of "The Old North State" and the music as collected and arranged were officially adopted as the state song, the State of North Carolina invested in a plate. This plate was used in printing the words and music in bulletins for distribution to public schools, public libraries of the state, and many religious, civic, and commercial organizations desiring copies of the state song.

Further development in the history of "The Old North State" occurred in 1927 when Major P. W. Price, musical director of North Carolina State College, had the song arranged for bands. A. B. Andrews of Raleigh financed the preparation of the song for complete band instrumentation and had copies sent to members of state institutions and bands throughout the United States.

The United Daughters of the Confederacy through their historian, Mrs. John H. Anderson, were also active in promoting a widespread interest in the singing of the state song.

During 1941–1942, the North Carolina Federation of Women's Clubs, through the courtesy of Mrs. A. C. Burnham, chairman of the Music Division of the State Federation, published and distributed 10,000 copies of an eight-page leaflet containing songs and readings for civic and patriotic meetings in the National Defense program. Included in this leaflet were the words and music of "The Old North State."

History source: "The Good Old North State," *The State*, October 1973.

STATE SONG

By an act of the General Assembly of 1927, the song known as "The Old North State" was legally adopted as the official song of the State of North Carolina.

THE OLD NORTH STATE

(Traditional air as sung in 1926)

North Dakota

"North Dakota Hymn"

The State Song of North Dakota, "North Dakota Hymn," words by James W. Foley and music by Dr. C. S. Putnam, was copyrighted in 1927.

Miss Minnie Nielson, then State Superinten dent of Public Instruction, requested James W. Foley, generally known and beloved as the poet of North Dakota, to write a song about North Dakota that schoolchildren could sing. A group of people, including Miss Nielson and Mr. Foley, were traveling in western North Dakota and, having come from Dickinson, they stopped for the night at the Park Hotel in Watford City. After the others retired for the evening, Mr. Foley remained in the hotel lobby to write, using the hotel's stationery. Part of Miss Nielson's program of education was to promote the idea of Americanization, and with this concept in mind Mr. Foley wrote the hymn and adapted it to the tune of Haydn's Austrian National Anthem. He handed Miss Nielson the first draft stating, "Here is your song." It was inscribed:

To Miss Minnie J. Nielson
State Superintendent
Watford City, Oct. 18, 1926
—James W. Foley

Dr. C. S. Putnam, who was head of the music department at Agricultural College in Fargo, North Dakota, was so impressed by the appropriateness of the words that he was inspired to compose music for the hymn. One story told is that someone showed him the copy of the hymn during orchestra practice, and that as soon as possible he left practice, went to his office, and paced the floor until the music came to him.

This hymn honors North Dakota, having words written by a state poet, music from a well-respected composer, and a dedication offering tribute to a devoted woman educator whose power and influence are marked by the evidence of her service to the people of North Dakota.

The "North Dakota Hymn" became the official song of North Dakota on March 15, 1947.

History compiled by Hladczuk and Hladczuk.

2
North Dakota Hymn
Words by
JAMES W. FOLEY
MIXED VOICES
Music by
Dr. C. S. PUTNAM
Moderato ♩ = M.M. 72
MIXED CHORUS
1 North Da - ko - ta,
2 Hear thy loy - al
3 On - ward, on-ward,
4 God of free-dom,
North Da - ko - ta, With thy prair - ies wide and free,
child - ren sing - ing, Songs of hap - pi - ness and praise,
on - ward go - ing, Light of cour - age in thine eyes,
all vic - to - rious, Give us Souls se - rene and strong,
All thy sons and daugh-ters love thee, Fair - est state from sea to
Far and long the ech-oes ring - ing Through the vast-ness of thy
Sweet the winds a - bove thee blow - ing, Green thy fields and fair thy
Strength to make the fu - ture glo - rious Keep the ech - o of our
Copyright 1927 by Dr. C. S. Putnam, State Collage, Fargo, N.D.

3
sea; North Da - ko - ta, North Da - ko - ta,
ways_ North Da - ko - ta, North Da - ko - ta,
skies. North Da - ko - ta, North Da - ko - ta,
song; North Da - ko - ta, North Da - ko - ta,
Here we pledge our-selves to thee. North Da - ko - ta,
We will serve thee all our days. North Da - ko - ta,
Brave the Soul that in thee lies. North Da - ko - ta,
In our hearts for - ev - er long. North Da - ko - ta,
North Da - ko - ta, Here we pledge our-selves to thee.
North Da - ko - ta, We will serve thee all our days.
North Da - ko - ta, Brave the Soul that in thee lies.
North Da - ko - ta, In our hearts for - ev - er long.
North Dakota Hymn 2 Mixed V.

Ohio

"Beautiful Ohio"

The music to "Beautiful Ohio" was written by Mary Earl (a pseudonym for Robert King), and the lyrics were written by Ballard MacDonald. "Beautiful Ohio" was adopted as the official State Song of Ohio in 1969.

Ballard MacDonald was born in either Portland, Oregon, or San Francisco, California—the records are confused on this point. He attended Princeton University and the Sorbonne. Later, he lived in Paris and London. While in Europe, Mr. MacDonald began writing songs, which he continued doing upon his return to the United States. Among his accomplishments, Ballard MacDonald wrote lyrics for stage works such as "The Boys and Betty" and "The Matinee Idol." His best known piece is "The Trail of the Lonesome Pine."

He died in Forest Hills, New York, on November 17, 1935.

Robert King was born on September 20, 1862, in New York. His career included work as an errand boy, vaudeville performer, salesperson, writer, and composer. Mary Earl was but one of many pseudonyms under which Robert A. King wrote. Among other songs, he wrote "Apple Blossoms," "Anona," "Why Did I Kiss That Girl," and "I Scream, You Scream, We All Scream for Ice Cream."

Robert A. King died in New York on April 14, 1932.

In 1989, Bill #33 was introduced and passed changing the original words of "Beautiful Ohio." The new words were written by an attorney, Mr. Wilbert McBride, of Youngstown, Ohio. The new words have not been reproduced here, however, because all attempts to reach Mr. McBride and/or to ascertain copyright ownership have been to no avail. Mr. McBride could neither be reached in Youngstown nor through the Ohio State Bar Association. Further, the attorney registration office of the Supreme Court of Ohio has informed us that the last, inactive registration that they have recorded for Mr. McBride is dated 1991.

History compiled by Hladczuk and Hladczuk.

 "Beautiful Ohio" has been officially adopted as the Official State Song Of Ohio

Beautiful Ohio

Lyric by
BALLARD MACDONALD

Music by
MARY EARL

Moderate Waltz Tempo

mf

C

Chorus

G7

Drift - ing with the cur - rent down a moon - lit stream

C

While a - bove the heav - ens in their glo - ry gleam

C Dm7 G7

And the stars on high

Beautiful Ohio-3

Beautiful Ohio-3

Oklahoma

"Oklahoma"

Our state has produced far more writers in various fields than most folks know about. Time makes that newsprint fade away and spotlights no longer flash, while that old man with the scythe gets into action.

One of these persons was Lynn Riggs, born three miles from Claremore on August 31, 1899, who died in Santa Fe just before his 54th birth anniversary. You probably remember him best for writing a play called *Green Grow the Lilacs*, which Richard Rodgers and Oscar Hammerstein II made into the popular musical *Oklahoma!*

Lynn had so much going for him. He scrabbled a lot to get started in what he really wanted to do in life, but when he reached success, and with it the money to live as he wanted to, time ran out on him. His royalties from the long Broadway run of *Oklahoma!* let him live in style, although his preferred style was not ostentatious.

Lynn's father, William G. Riggs, died in 1951. He was of English and Scotch-Irish extraction. Mrs. Riggs was one-eighth Cherokee, a fact Will Rogers commented upon frequently when he lauded the writer from Claremore. The Riggs family were ranchers.

The young man attended the former Oklahoma Military Academy at Claremore and the University of Oklahoma. He majored in English, which later permitted him to teach English at OU a couple of years. The feeling for poetry that grew within him also began to show. A volume entitled *The Iron Dish* contained many poems written for *Smart Set* magazine, then edited by George Gene Nathan.

In an interlude between graduating from OMA in 1917 and going to OU in 1920, Lynn tried several things. He worked briefly for the *Wall Street Journal* in New York, sold books in Macy's literary department for a time, tried Hollywood as an extra, and—to eat—was a proofreader on the *Los Angeles Times*.

His creative work while at OU led to a Guggenheim Fellowship for a year's study abroad—or whatever else you wanted to do so long as you got across that whale pasture to do it—and that's where his masterpiece of a play was written. That was in Italy, although he spent some time in France.

This is somewhat ahead of the chronology. *Lilacs* was one of 18 plays that Riggs wrote, of which nine had a territorial, or early statehood, locale in Oklahoma. It was a bell ringer. He did several one acts and longer plays.

The Lilacs was remolded into a play for the Theater Guild and starred Franchot Tone. It was produced by the Guild in New York and rated as one of the ten best plays of 1931. That was about a year after we had the pleasure of becoming acquainted with Riggs.

Robert Littrell, drama critic for the *New York World*, said about *Lilacs* that it "was full of rich, free humor, salty poetry and some reckless tenderness that was America before she was tamed and civilized by fences, mortgages, and chain grocery stores.

"The spirit of the frontier is there . . . not only in the racy, simple language, but in what its people think and do. It is a glorious breath of fresh air, making those of us who live beside subways long—for way down inside us we are still Americans—for something lost out of our lives, something long ago and far away."

Riggs's *Russet Mantle* was the first hit of the season in 1936. The setting was Santa Fe. Robert Benchley, drama critic among other writings, praised that play. There was *The Domino Parlor*, which Lionel Barrymore said was the best play he had read in 20 years. Another play, *Roadside*, folded after 11 performances, but it started Ralph Bellamy on his long career.

There were some others such as *The Lonesome West*, *Verdigris Primitive*, *Borned in Texas*, and *Sump 'n Like Wings*. Once Lynn had four plays on Broadway the same time.

There was a stint in Hollywood writing movie scenarios. Lynn didn't think this was exactly his cup of tea—doctoring someone else's writing—but after his success in the legitimate theater money beckoned. One script that he did was *The Plainsman*, starring Gary Cooper. Another was *The Garden of Allah*. In World War II, he wrote training films as a Signal Corps sergeant.

During that fracas, four of us were put on temporary duty for two weeks in Washington and one in New York, with the Office of War Information, and to this day we don't know why. But we did it and then went to a staging area. But in that week in the big city two of us went to see *Oklahoma!* and alternated standing up places in the theater. Only "seats" left. It was worth it.

When the movie version of that musical was made, we went to New York on the promotion with Governor and Mrs. Gary, Dr. C. Q. Smith, and the Oklahoma City University Surrey Singers. Shirley Jones and Gordon McCrae, the stars, were with us on one eventful social session, as were Rodgers and Hammerstein. What an evening—out on Long Island Sound at the producer's estate. Just like a movie set.

There was an attempt made to do something of a memorial nature for Lynn, at Claremore, [a bit later.] An official act was passed by the legislature and the governor appointed some of us to the Lynn Riggs Memorial Commission. Both the legislature and the governor were careful not to attach any money to this venture. We never got very far. Rodgers and Hammerstein did see that models of the musical's stage sets were sent to Claremore. They may be in the public library there now.

History written by Roy P. Stewart, columnist. History appears courtesy of Oklahoma Cattlemen's Association, Inc., publisher of *Cowman,* in which this brief history originally appeared as a column entitled "Country Boy" in the August 1984 issue.

2
Oklahoma
Words by
OSCAR HAMMERSTEIN II
Music by
RICHARD RODGERS
VOICE
Piano
Brand new state! Brand new state, gon-na treat you
great! Gon-na give you bar-ley, car-rots and per-
ta-ters, Pas-ture fer the cat-tle, Spin-ach and ter-may-ters!
Flow-ers on the prair-ie where the June bugs zoom, Plen-ty of air and
mf marcato
* Names of chords for Ukulele and Banjo.
Symbols for Guitar.

3
F6
G7
plen'-y of room, Plen'-y of room to swing a rope!
cresc.
C
Dmi.7
C
F
C
Dmi.7
C
Ami.
G7
Plen'-y of heart and plen'-y of hope.
f
mf cresc.
C
Refrain (lustily)
F
C
G7
Gdim.
O k - la-hom-a, where the wind comes sweep-in' down the
mf-f
G7 (sus.4)
G7
C9
F6
Fmi.6
plain And the wav - in' wheat can sure smell sweet When the

4
C
C (add F)
A7
D7
G7
C
wind comes right be-hind the rain.
O
f
F
C
G7
Gdim.
G7 (sus.4)
G7
-k - la-hom-a, Ev-'ry night my hon-ey lamb and I sit a-
C9
F6
Fmi.6
C
G7
lone and talk and watch a hawk mak-in' laz-y cir-cles in the
C
F
C
sky. We know we be-long to the land

5
G D7 G9 Emi. G7 C
And the land we be - long to is grand! And when we say
fp
D7 G D7
(yell)
Yeeow! A - yip - i - o - ee ay! We're
cresc.
C E7 Ami. Ami.7 D7
on - ly say - in' You're do - in' fine, Ok - la - hom - a! Ok - la -
C G7 1. C A♭7 G7 2. C
hom - a O. K. K.
sf

Oregon

"Oregon, My Oregon"

Anyone remember singing a song by Buchanan and Murtagh? If you went to school in Oregon within the last 30 years, the chances are you have sung it and probably still remember part or all of the words and music. The chances are also that the names John Andrew Buchanan and Henry B. Murtagh mean nothing more to you than the names of any two strangers in the telephone directory.

But the one thing put together by Buchanan and Murtagh has been sung more times by more people than any other song composed in Oregon. The song is "Oregon, My Oregon," the state's official song. Since the early '20s, nearly every school child in Oregon has sung it.

Buchanan was a municipal judge who liked to write poetry. Murtagh was a professional musician—a theater organist in the silent movie days when the artist at the keyboard of the mighty Wurlitzer drew billing almost equal with the picture.

The judge's lyrics and the organist's music came together as the winning entry in a competition sponsored by the Society of Oregon Composers in 1920. The music was published later the same year with an endorsement by the state superintendent of public instruction. In 1927 the legislature made it the official state song.

It is reprinted, words and music, in every new edition of the Oregon *Bluebook.*

Judge Buchanan died in 1936 at his home in Astoria. A number of years ago, Murtagh left Portland, where he had been at several theaters and lastly at the United Artists, for Los Angeles. Old associates here have not heard of him since World War II days, when he traveled through Portland with a bond drive group.

History by Paul Hauser, staff writer of *The Oregonian,* printed here by permission of *Northwest Rotogravure Magazine,* January 8, 1986.

OREGON STATE SONG

SECRETARY OF STATE
BARBARA ROBERTS
Salem, Oregon 97310

SED 123SG
Rev. 1/7/85

Pennsylvania

"Pennsylvania"

The writing of the song "Pennsylvania" in 1967 was motivated by the fact that the state was one of a few that had not adopted an "official" song. An additional incentive was the urging by a Philadelphia newspaper columnist to adopt such a song to celebrate the up-coming Bi-Centennial Year—1976. To achieve such a lofty objective, a song in the anthem vein seemed most appropriate. Having completed the lyrics, I gave them to my long-time cowriter, Ronnie Bonner, to compose the music. A sheet music edition of our completed work was published in 1967. In 1969 the song was nominated for a Freedoms Foundation Award.

Over the years, many efforts were made in the state capitol to adopt an "official" song but none reached fruition. It wasn't until 1988 when State Representative Frank L. Oliver came up with a plan to form a committee of music professionals to select a song without legislative influence. Our song was among the over two hundred which the state had accumulated over the years. Being totally unaware of this latest effort, we were completely surprised when notified of the selection of our song by this committee.

On June 8, 1988, the song was performed live in the Harrisburg Capitol rotunda before a gathering which included the House Committee. After the performance the song was unanimously approved, thus overcoming the years of political wrangling and partisan bickering.

On November 29, 1990, "Pennsylvania" was adopted as the official song of Pennsylvania.

History courtesy Edward A. Khoury,
co-composer of "Pennsylvania."

PENNSYLVANIA

Gm7 C7 F Dm7 Gm6 A7
Ty - ran - ny de - cried, 'Til the bell of in - de -
Free- dom to pro - claim, May the voic -es of to -
Dm Dm7 G7 C7
pend-ence filled the coun - try - side. PENN-SYL -
mor - row glo - ri - fy your name. PENN-SYL -
F F9
VA - NIA, PENN-SYL - VA - NIA, May your fu - ture
VA - NIA, PENN-SYL - VA - NIA, May your fu - ture
cresc.
B♭ D7 Gm F Fdim F B♭ B♭m6
be filled with hon - or ev - er - last - ing
be filled with hon - or ev - er - last - ing
1. 2.
F C7 F C7 F F6
as your his - to - ry. PENN-SYL-
as your his - to - ry.
poco rall.
mf
sf
PENNSYLVANIA (2)

Rhode Island

"Rhode Island's It for Me"

The inspiration for the state song of Rhode Island came about in an interesting, if not ironic way.

A local comedian named Charlie Hall had created a comedy cabaret called "Ocean State Follies" in 1992 (and is still running at the time of this printing). It was a show that poked good-natured fun at Rhode Island's celebrities, politics, and politicians. One politician who had more than his share of "stage time" was the mayor of the capital city, Vincent "Buddy" Cianci.

One night Buddy happened to run into Hall at the local jazz club. After praising Hall's comic talents, he dared Hall to write a positive song about the state instead of satirizing the home that Buddy so dearly loved.

Hall went right home and took on the challenge. Within days, he had scribbled down lyrics that were inspired by the natural beauty of the state and its residents. Next, Hall went to his senior cast member from "Ocean State Follies," Maria Day, a singer and music teacher. She wrote a lovely melody for the words that Hall had written. "Follies" musical director Kathryn Chester finished off the product with a beautiful arrangement.

"Rhode Island's It For Me" was added into the line-up of the show, and Rhode Islanders quickly embraced it. Four years and hundreds of performances later, David Bates, a state senator, took it upon himself to make "RI's It" the official state song. Since there was already a state song on the books, the RI legislature voted to make that one the official state march, paving the way for "RI's It" as the new state song. In the fall of 1996, after successful votes in the State Senate and House of Representatives, "Rhode Island's It For Me" became the Official State Song of the "Biggest Little State of the Union."

History courtesy of comedian Charlie Hall.

Rhode Island's It For Me

Lyrics by Charlie Hall   Music by Maria Day   Arrangement by Kathryn Chester

2.
Ab Bb Eb Eb Ebmaj7 Ab
boats that line the docks. I see the lighthouse flicker-ing to help the sail-ors
Bb cresc. Ab/Bb Ab Bb
CHORUS
see There's a place for every-one, Rhode Is-land's It For Me! Rhode-
cresc.
mf
Ebmaj7 subito Ab Bb
Is-land, Oh, Rhode Is-land sur-round-ed by the sea, Some peo-ple roam the earth
Subito p
Ab/Bb Ab Bb Eb Ebmaj7
for home, Rhode Is-land's It For Me! 2. I love the fresh Oc-to-ber days, The
dim
p

3.
A♭
B♭
A♭/B♭
buzz on Col - lege Hill,
Art that moves an eye to tear a jew'ler's special skill
E♭
E♭maj 7
Ic - i - cles re - fract the sun, Snow fal - ling grace - ful - ly, Some
sempre p
A♭/B♭
D.S. al Coda
Coda
Cm
mf
search for a place that's warm, Rhode Is - land's It For Me!
3. The sky-line pierc - ing
Cm(+7)
Cm7
Cmb
F7
B♭7
Pro - vi - dence. The state house dome so rare,
Res - i - dents who speak their minds, No long - er un - a -

4.
B
subito f
E
Emaj7
cresc
ware
cresc
f
Yes, Roger Williams would be proud to
cresc
f
subito f
cresc.
A
B
A/B
A
f
B
see his col-on-y So, don't sell short this pre-cious port, Rhode Is-land's It For
E
CHORUS
Emaj7
A
Me! Rhode-Is-land, Oh, Rhode Is-land sur-round-ed by the sea, Some
B
A/B
A
B
E
peo-ple roam the earth for home, Rhode Is-land's It For Me! Rhode Is-land, Oh, Rhode

5.
Emaj7
A
B
mf
Is - land, sur-round-ed by the sea, Some peo-ple roam the earth for home, Rhode
ritard
rit.
mf
A
B
E
Emaj7
A
mp
Is - land's It For Me!
Broadly
mp
rit.
Broadly
Tempo primo
rit.
Am
E
p
pp
8va

South Carolina

"Carolina"

There are three state songs recognized as official songs for the state of South Carolina. The first song, "Carolina," was a Confederate poem written by Henry Timrod, with original music composed by Anne Custis Burgess.

Henry Timrod was born December 8, 1828, in Charleston, South Carolina. His father, William Henry, died as a result of his service in the Seminole War, leaving his wife, the former Thyrza Prince, in poverty. Nonetheless, Henry spent two years studying the classics at Franklin College (later to become the University of Georgia in Athens), then he read law in the office of James L. Petigru in Charleston. Henry renewed his classical studies in order to become a college professor but instead taught school for a term at Bluffton and became a tutor on a Carolina plantation. During this time he also wrote and published poetry and prose in magazines, periodicals, and newspapers.

The impending hostilities between the North and South inspired in him many impassioned war poems, which earned him the title of "laureate of the Confederacy" because his words so strongly stirred the South. In 1861, he wrote his elaborate ode "Ethnogenesis," which was the first of his noteworthy series of war poems. "Carolina" was considered the high-water mark of his series.

He spent a short time in the service and was discharged from the Confederate Army of the West in December of 1862 due to contracting tuberculosis.

Kate Goodwin and he married on February 16, 1864, in Columbia, South Carolina. They had a son who was born on Christmas Eve in 1864 but who died in October at the age of ten months. A year and a day after the marriage, the city of Columbia was burned and Timrod's livelihood as part proprietor and associate editor of the *South Carolinian* was destroyed. His life became a tragedy as he was brought to the verge of starvation, selling his family's belongings in order to eat. He continued to write, but he became ill and died close to his 39th birthday on October 7, 1867. (Although his gravestone in Trinity Churchyard in Columbia has his birth year engraved as 1829, his father's notebook has his birth recorded as 1828.)

Henry Timrod made a small but valuable contribution to American literature. His friends attempted to perpetuate his fame after his death. Hayne Simms edited *The Poems of Henry Timrod* in 1873. Other works appeared, and in 1898 the Timrod Memorial Association was founded and in a year's time inspired a widespread interest in Timrod and his work.

Anne Custis Burgess was born on January 22, 1874, in Mayesville in Sumter County, South Carolina. She was a musician and a poet, one of three daughters and five sons of Dr. Thomas L. Burgess and Frances Mayes Burgess. She died at age 36 on October 15, 1910.

She attended Memminger School in Charleston and received her music degree from Converse College in 1901. After a year of private study with Mrs. E. E. Ayers in Hagerstown, Maryland, she taught music in Summerton, Williamston, Winthrop College, and the Thornwell orphanage.

While teaching in Williamston, Anne heard Timrod's verses set to the music of "Maryland"

and was led to compose original music for the verses. After the first public presentation at a grade-school commencement in 1905, she decided to submit her work to several music authorities and critics. Among the many who endorsed her effort was W. A. Courtenay, who had been a friend and admirer of Timrod's.

The song was published in 1906 by Smithdeal Music Company of Columbia, was sung at many important public occasions, and received official endorsement at state and local functions. It was well known by the time it was adopted as state song by resolution of the General Assembly of the South Carolina Legislature on February 11, 1911.

"South Carolina: The Palmetto State"

In 1972, "South Carolina: The Palmetto State" was officially recognized as a state song by resolution of the General Assembly of the South Carolina Legislature. Lily Strickland, a distinguished American composer, composed the music in 1958 for several verses of Harry Russell Wilkins's poem. The two met in 1941 in Union City, South Carolina, when she was the Honor Guest on the program at the Annual Convention of the South Carolina Federation of Music Clubs. They became friends and Lily wrote music for a number of his poems.

Lily Strickland was born on January 28, 1884, in Anderson, South Carolina, at Echo Hall, the home of Judge and Mrs. J. Pinckney Reed, her maternal grandparents. Her father was Charlton Hines Strickland and her mother was the former Teresa Hammond Reed. She studied music at Converse College in Spartanburg from 1901 to 1904 and in 1905 received a scholarship to the Institute of Musical Art in New York (now the Juilliard School of Music). There she studied piano, orchestration, theory, and composition for several years.

She and Joseph Cortenay Anderson, also a South Carolinian, married in 1912. He was studying and teaching at Columbia University in New York City. In 1920 she accompanied her husband to Calcutta, India, where they lived for nine and one-half years. They traveled in India, Burma, the Philippines, China, Japan, and principal capital cities of Europe. She continued to compose and in 1924 was conferred a Doctor of Music degree from Converse College.

From 1930 to 1942, they lived in New York State. In 1942 they moved to Charleston, South Carolina. During their time in Charleston, the Charleston Symphony Orchestra performed her orchestral suite "Charleston Sketches."

Their next move was in 1948 to Hendersonville, North Carolina, where she continued to compose until her death in 1958. She was buried in historic Silver Brook Cemetery in Anderson, South Carolina.

On August 10, 1885, Harry Russell Wilkins was born to Mr. and Mrs. Robert Russell Wilkins in Gaffney, South Carolina. He graduated from the Citadel in Charleston in 1908 and became a member of the faculty at Porter Military Academy there for two years. Later he moved to Greenville, South Carolina, and went into the real estate business. In 1923, after his father's death, he moved back to Gaffney to be with his mother. There he became active in the Chamber of Commerce and the Rotary Club. He sold insurance, but after his mother's death in 1934, he moved the agency to Spartanburg where he lived for 30 years and retired as a district manager.

He was a charter member of the Rotary Club of Greenville, a member of the local Association of Life Underwriters, and served as president several times. He was also on the board of directors of the South Carolina Association of Life Underwriters; was a member of the First Baptist Church, the men's Baraca Class, the Historical Society of Charleston, the Spartanburg County Historical Association, the Greenville County Historical Society, and the American Society of Composers, Authors, and Publishers (ASCAP); and was active in the Community Chest and the United Fund.

Several of his poems were set to music by various composers besides Lily Strickland. Two songs written by different composers were "Kings Mountain Battlefield" and "Cowpens Battleground." During World War II, he wrote a poem titled "We Salute the Philippines" to express admiration and gratitude to the people of the Philippines for being loyal and courageous allies of the United States of America. Several verses of the poem were set to patriotic music composed by Alejandro del Rosario, then director of the department of music of the Philippines government in Manila. It was published there under the title "God Bless the Philippines."

Harry Wilkins lived to the age of 91 and was buried in Oakland Cemetery at Gaffney in 1976.

"South Carolina on My Mind"

"South Carolina on My Mind" was designated an official state song by legislative act of the South Carolina General Assembly in 1984. Hank Martin and Buzz Arledge, both native South Carolinians, created, sang, and recorded the song, which was distributed as a record by Palmetto Records of Nashville, Tennessee, to radio stations and which was used in other advertising and promotional materials by television and other media.

The South Carolina Department of Parks, Recreation, and Tourism initially encouraged Martin and Arledge and the result of this encouragement was widespread use of their song by radio stations nationwide. The song was one of ten songs on the *South Carolina on My Mind* album produced and recorded by Martin and Arledge.

The musicians sang the song at several South Carolina Governor's Conferences, at the halftime show of a University of South Carolina football game, the Pendleton Spring Jubilee, and other major events. It has been used as a theme song at national conventions and by other programs, including the University of South Carolina basketball team. Organizations used the song for entertainment and promotional purposes, and because of its popularity, this beautiful, inspiring ballad was officially designated a state song, joining the two other state songs.

History compiled by Hladczuk and Hladcuk.

2

Carolina

Words by TIMROD

Music by A. C. B.

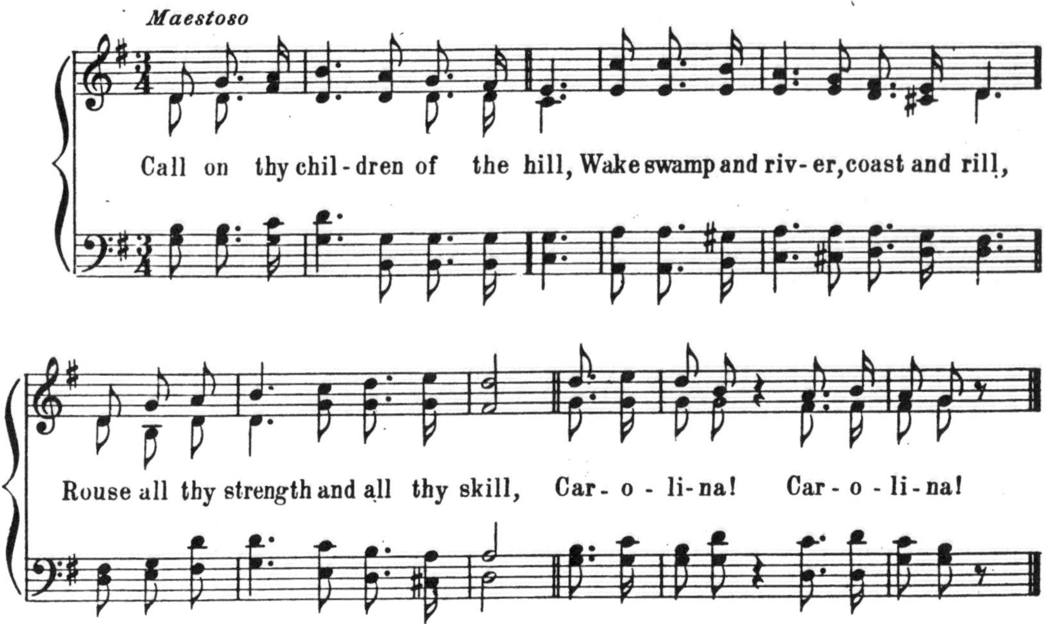

1.
*Call on thy children of the hill,
Wake swamp and river, coast and rill,
Rouse all thy strength and all thy skill,
Carolina! Carolina!

2.
Hold up the glories of thy dead;
Say how thy elder children bled,
And point to Eutaw's battle-bed,
Carolina! Carolina!

3.
Thy skirts indeed the foe may part,
Thy robe be pierced with sword and dart,
They shall not touch thy noble heart,
Carolina! Carolina!

4.
Throw thy bold banner to the breeze!
Front with thy ranks the threatening seas
Like thine own proud armorial trees,
Carolina! Carolina!

5.
Girt with such wills to do and bear,
Assured in right, and mailed in prayer,
Thou wilt not bow thee to despair,
Carolina! Carolina!

**These stanzas are selected as forming an appropriate patriotic song for our school-children.*

3

CAROLINA

1.

The despot treads thy sacred sands,
Thy pines give shelter to his bands,
Thy sons stand by with idle hands,
Carolina!
He breathes at ease thy airs of balm,
He scorns the lances of thy palm;
Oh,who shall break thy craven calm,
Carolina!
Thy ancient fame is growing dim,
A spot is on thy garment's rim;
Give to the winds thy battle hymn,
Carolina!

2.

Call on thy children of the hill,
Wake swamp and river,coast and rill,
Rouse all thy strength and all thy skill,
Carolina!
Cite wealth and science,trade and art,
Touch with thy fire the cautious mart,
And pour thee through the people's heart,
Carolina!
Till even the coward spurns his fears,
And all thy fields and fens and meres
Shall bristle like thy palm with spears,
Carolina!

3.

Hold up the glories of thy dead;
Say how thy elder children bled,
And point to Eutaw's battle-bed,
Carolina!
Tell how the patriot's soul was tried,
And what his dauntless breast defied;
How Rutledge ruled and Laurens died,
Carolina!
Cry!till thy summons,heard at last,
Shall fall like Marion's bugle-blast
Re-echoed from the haunted past,
Carolina!

4.

I hear a murmur as of waves
That grope their way through sunless caves,
Like bodies struggling in their graves,
Carolina!
And now it deepens;slow and grand
It swells, as,rolling to the land,
An ocean broke upon thy strand,
Carolina!
Shout!let it reach the startled Huns!
And roar with all thy festal guns!
It is the answer of thy sons,
Carolina!

5.

They will not wait to hear thee call;
From Sachem's Head to Sumter's wall
Resounds the voice of hut and hall,
Carolina!
No!thou hast not a stain,they say,
Or none save what the battle day
Shall wash in seas of blood away,
Carolina!
Thy skirts indeed the foe may part,
Thy robe be pierced with sword and dart,
They shall not touch thy noble heart,
Carolina!

6.

Ere thou shalt own the tyrant's thrall
Ten times ten thousand men must fall;
Thy corpse may hearken to his call,
Carolina!
When,by thy bier,in mournful throngs
The women chant thy mortals wrongs,
'Twill be their own funereal songs,
Carolina!
From thy dead breast by ruffians trod
No helpless child shall look to God;
All shall be safe beneath thy sod,
Carolina!

7.

Girt with such wills to do and bear,
Assured in right,and mailed in prayer,
Thou wilt not bow thee to despair,
Carolina!
Throw thy bold banner to the breeze!
Front with thy ranks the threatening seas
Like thine own proud armorial trees,
Carolina!
Fling down thy gauntlet to the Huns,
And roar thy challenge from thy guns;
Then leave the future to thy sons,
Carolina!

2

South Carolina

The Palmetto State

Words by
HARRY RUSSELL WILKINS

Music by
LILY STRICKLAND, 1884-1958

If preferred, sing the REFRAIN after the 2nd and 4th verses only.

SOUTH CAROLINA ON MY MIND

Words & Music by
HANK MARTIN

South Dakota

"Hail! South Dakota"

"Hail! South Dakota" was adopted by the state legislature March 5, 1943, as the official song of the State of South Dakota.

The state song of South Dakota was originally written as a part of the march, "The Round-Up." "The Round-Up" march was written in honor of the Tri-State Round-up of Belle Fourche, South Dakota, in the year 1926. The words to "Hail! South Dakota" were written to the Trio of "The Round-Up" march in the year 1927. This was the year President Coolidge spent the summer at the Summer White House, Custer State Park, in the Black Hills.

The Alcester Community Band led by Deecort Hammitt was playing at the Belle Fourche Round-up when the President and Mrs. Coolidge attended. To honor the President and Mrs. Coolidge, special words were written by Mr. Hammitt and sung to them by the Cowboy Quartet accompanied by the band. Mr. Hammitt received a personal letter of thanks from the President.

In 1933–1934 the State of South Dakota was musically represented by Mr. Hammitt and the Alcester Community Band at the Century of Progress Worlds Fair in Chicago, Illinois.

Mr. Hammitt was born in Spencer, South Dakota, and wrote his first South Dakota song, "South Dakota Rag," in 1913. In the fifties he wrote "The South Dakota Waltz," which was recorded by Ken Harris on ERIN Records. Other songs were "Sweet Little Pilgrim" published by Handy Bros. Music Co. New York (W. C. Handy—"St. Louis Blues"); "You Ought to Be Kissed" and "Let's Linger on in Avalon," recorded by the Bill Pannell Orchestra; "To a Prairie Lullaby," featured by the Lawrence Welk Orchestra. "The Round-up" march has been played by bands worldwide including the U.S. Navy Band on NBC radio, Ringling Bros. Shows, Swedish Bank (Kost, Sweden), Stanford University Band, Herbert L. Clarke and the Long Beach Municipal Band.

Deecort and Bessie Jane Hammitt (his wife) had seven sons who served in the military service, five of them during World War II. There were eleven children—eight boys and three girls. All living at this writing. Mr. Hammitt passed on in 1970 and his wife in 1975.

History courtesy of Orlin Hammitt.

WINNER OF STATE SONG CONTEST — THE CHOICE OF THE PEOPLE

The Selected South Dakota Song for All Occasions

"HAIL! SOUTH DAKOTA"

A Great State of The Land

Words and Music
by
DEECORT HAMMITT

Play in Snappy March Time

Intro.

f

Voice *Sing with spirit*

fz

mf

1. Hail! South Da - ko - ta, A great state of the land, ___ Health, wealth and beau - ty, That's what
2. Come where the sun shines, And where life's worth your while, ___ You won't be here long, 'Till you'll
3. Hail! South Da - ko - ta, The state we love the best, ___ Land of our fa - thers, Build - ers

8

makes her grand; She has her Black Hills, And mines with gold so rare, And with her scen' - ry,
wear a smile; No state's so health - y, And no folk quite so true, To South Da - ko - ta.
of the west; Home of the Bad - lands, And Rush - more's age - less shrine, Black Hills and prai - ries,
(Hills, farms and prai - ries,
No state can com - pare. pare.
We all wel - come you. you.
Farm - land and Sun - shine.
Blessed with bright Sun - shine.)
fz
QUARTETTE, MIXED VOICES AND
BAND ARRANGEMENTS AVAILABLE
RAYNER, DALHEIM & CO. MUSIC PRINTERS CHICAGO
Free rights will be granted to Schools, Churches, Newspapers, Broadcasting Stations and Musical Organizations in South Dakota.

Tennessee

"My Homeland, Tennessee"

"My Homeland, Tennessee" was written by Roy Lamont Smith (music) and Nell Grayson Taylor (lyrics).

Roy Lamont Smith was born in Freemont, Nebraska. He studied music at the Royal Conservatory in Vienna, Austria, and then joined the Cadek Conservatory of the University of Chattanooga, in Chattanooga, Tennessee, in 1904. Some of Professor Smith's more popular compositions were "Fairy Tale Suite," "Meadow Lark," and "I Sing to Thee." Professor Smith retired in 1942 and moved to California, where he died on February 7, 1946.

Nell Grayson Taylor was born and raised in Chattanooga, Tennessee, but later moved to Memphis and, in June of 1917, graduated as a nurse. Almost immediately thereafter she enrolled in the Memphis Hospital Unit Perluch. In January of 1918 she was sent to the American Headquarters' Hospital in Chaumont, France. She published her first poem, "The Wooden Crosses," on December 18, 1918, in *Stars and Stripes.*

After the war, Nell Grayson Taylor returned home, where she eventually settled in Robertson County, Tennessee. It was there that she was advised that the Chattanooga Writers Club was looking for words for a state song. She wrote the lyrics in Springfield and Nashville, Tennessee.

"My Homeland, Tennessee" was adopted as a state song in 1925.

History compiled by Hladczuk and Hladczuk.

"When It's Iris Time in Tennessee"

"When It's Iris Time in Tennessee" was written by Willa Mae Waid while Miss Waid was a student at Peabody College in Nashville, Tennessee. It has been reported that while at Peabody College, Miss Waid collaborated with C. E. Branscombe in the writing of the song.

In 1935, "When It's Iris Time in Tennessee" was adopted as an official song of the state of Tennessee by the 69th General Assembly Chapter 154 of the Public Acts.

History compiled by Hladczuk and Hladczuk.

"My Tennessee"

Frances Hannah Tranum was born on a farm in upper east Tennessee. As a child, her favorite pastime was writing poems and setting them to the melodies that she created. She ran away from home at the age of 14. From then on, she pursued her education wherever and whenever the opportunity presented itself.

Mrs. Tranum stated that the lyrics came to her spontaneously, over the course of an hour, and were divinely inspired and guided. She wrote "My Tennessee" to inspire in the schoolchildren of Tennessee a greater love of and loyalty to state and country.

"My Tennessee" was adopted as a State Song of Tennessee in 1955 as a result of Senate Joint Resolution 35 of the 79th General Assembly.

History compiled by Hladczuk and Hladczuk.

"Tennessee Waltz"

"While driving back to Nashville from some dates in Texas, Redd Stewart and I were listening to the radio and heard Bill Monroe's 'Kentucky Waltz' and Redd remarked, 'It's odd no one ever did a "Tennessee Waltz," since we make our living on the Grand Ole Opry.'" On the back of an old-fashioned match box, the lyrics were composed. A song was born. Governor Frank Clement signed the bill officially on February 17, 1965, making it the Tennessee state song.

History written by song composer Pee Wee King. From *Sing Your Heart Out, Country Boy: Classic Country Songs and Their Inside Stories by the Men and Women Who Wrote Them* by Dorothy Horstman. © by the Country Music Foundation Press, Nashville, TN. Third Edition, 1996.

"Rocky Top"

"Rocky Top" has come a long way since its humble beginnings in Room 388 at the Gatlinburg Inn.

"We were in Gatlinburg in 1967 working on a project for Archie Campbell, Bob Ferguson, and Chet Atkins. We were writing a collection of songs for an album about the golden years of life," says Boudleaux [Bryant].

"We had worked and worked and worked. Suddenly Felice [Bryant] reneged. She sat down in the middle of the floor and refused to write another word.

"She said, 'Let's write something else. I'm tired of this.'"

"But Boudleaux wanted to keep at it," Felice interjects. "He kept saying, 'No, let's just keep going.' But I wouldn't do it."

"Boudleaux got mad. He picked up his guitar and strummed down real hard and said, 'OK, how's this: Rocky Top, you'll always be, home sweet home to me . . .'"

Felice got into the spirit of the song and they kept throwing lines back and forth.

"He accepted every dumb line I said, just to get it over with. And, 10 minutes later, it was finished, I had had my diversion and we went back to work."

But in the back of her mind, Felice kept thinking, "What a gem."

A few weeks later, back at home in Nashville, the Bryants got a call from Sonny Osborne of The Osborne Brothers.

"He said they were recording later that week and wondered if we had anything for him," says Boudleaux. "Sonny came over and we showed him five or six songs, but he didn't really flip out over anything. Then Felice said, 'How about that little song we wrote in Gatlinburg—Rocky Top?' I couldn't even remember what she was talking about."

Out of an unpacked box came the song that would later be named the official state song for Tennessee.

"Boudleaux played about four measures of the song and Sonny jumped up and said, 'I'll take it.' I said, 'Wait, he's not finished yet,' meaning he wasn't finished singing it, and Sonny said, 'I'll take it anyway.'"

"Felice says she knew that song was going to be a hit," says Boudleaux. "I never thought it would amount to much. But it was a little gem that fell out of heaven."

History by Sherri Gardner Howell.
Reprinted by permission of
The Knoxville News-Sentinel Co.

"Tennessee"

In 1992, by way of House Joint Resolution 744 of the 97th Tennessee General Assembly, "Tennessee," by Vivian Rorie, was adopted as an official state song.

Unfortunately, because all attempts to ascertain ownership and/or copyright have been to no avail, neither the music nor the lyrics have been reproduced here.

History compiled by Hladczuk and Hladczuk.

My Homeland, Tennessee

W.M.Co. 8251

3
pur - ple hills our cra - dle was; Thy fields our mo - ther breast. Be -
here be - fore their rap - tured eyes; In beau - teous ma - jes - ty: Out
no! the State where Jack - son sleeps, Shall ev - er peer - less be. We
neath thy sun - ny bend - ed skies, Our child-hood days were blessed.
spread the smi - ling val - leys of the wind - ing Ten - nes - see.
glo - ry in thy ma - jes - ty; Our home-land, Ten - nes - see.
O Ten - nes - see: Fair Ten - nes - see: Our
love for thee can nev - er die: Dear Home-land, Ten - nes - see.
My Homeland T. - 2

2

To My Mother

When It's Iris Time In Tennessee

When It's Iris Time In Tennessee - 3

4

When It's Iris Time In Tennessee - 3

My Tennessee

By FRANCES HANNAH TRANUM

More nat-ural beau - ty o'er the land From ev - 'ry stream,
The joys su - preme, you could be - stow The song of birds,
To do and dare, their deeds they gave Cour-age-ous - ly,
and val - ley green, His wond-'rous art is ev - er
the whis-p'ring trees, The low of herds, the hum of
with-out a fear, And won the name of vol - un -
seen, Ah, let my heart beat true to thee,
bees, It all comes back so dear to me,
teer, In sa-cred trust, let those who will,
And swell with pride for Ten - nes - see.
My child - hood home in Ten - nes - see.
By be - ing just, pre - serve it still.

4
CHORUS
p-f
Oh, Ten - nes - see, My Ten - nes - see,
Thy hills and vales are fair to see,
With moun - tains grand, and fer - tile lands,
There is no state more dear to me,
My Tennessee - 4

Thro oth - er climes, tho I may roam,
There will be times I'll long for home, In Ten-nes-
see, Fair Ten - nes - see, The land of my na -
tiv - i - ty Oh, Ten-nes, ty.
1
2
My Tennessee - 4

TENNESSEE WALTZ

Words and Music by
REDD STEWART and
PEE WEE KING

Tennessee Waltz - 2 - 1
1503TP2X

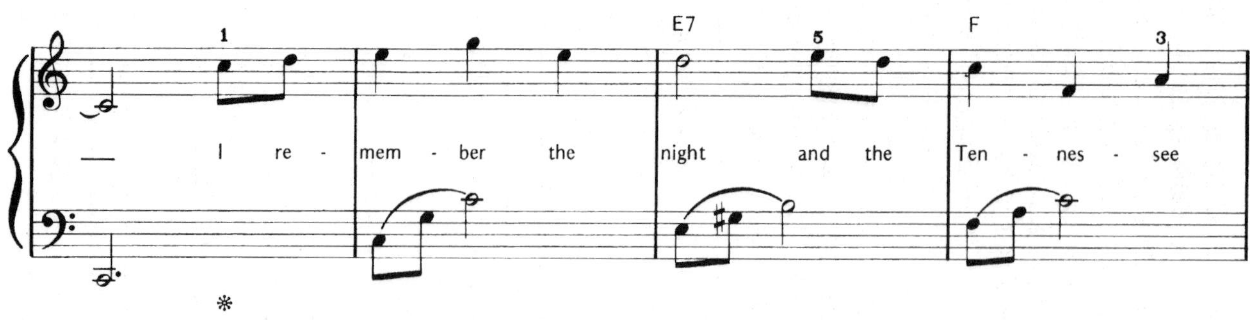
1
E7
5
F
3
I re - mem - ber the night and the Ten - nes - see

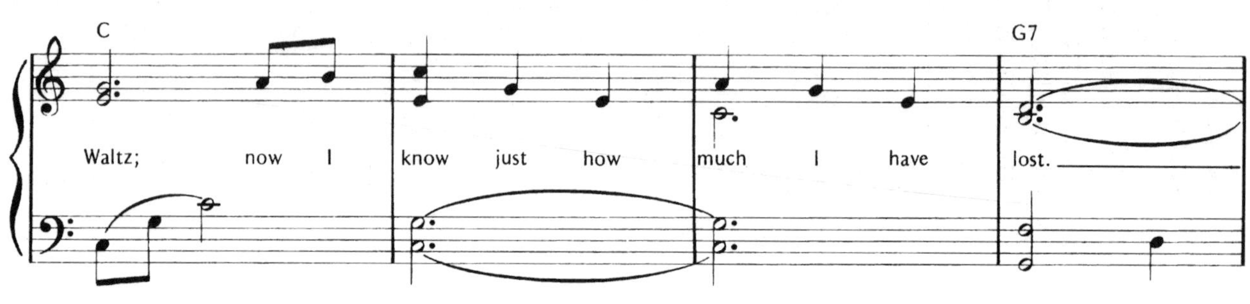
C
G7
Waltz; now I know just how much I have lost.

C
1
C7
Yes, I lost my lit - tle dar - ling the night they were

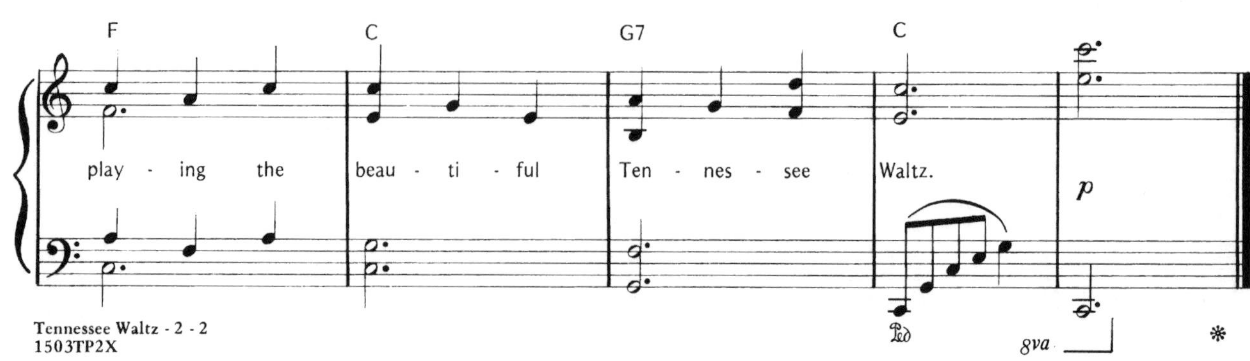
F
C
G7
C
play - ing the beau - ti - ful Ten - nes - see Waltz.
p
8va

2

ROCKY TOP

Words and Music by
BOUDLEAUX BRYANT and
FELICE BRYANT

Lively

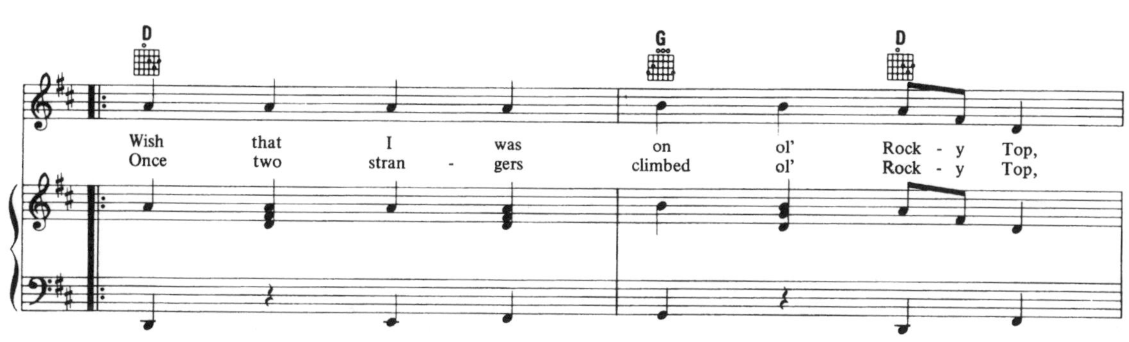

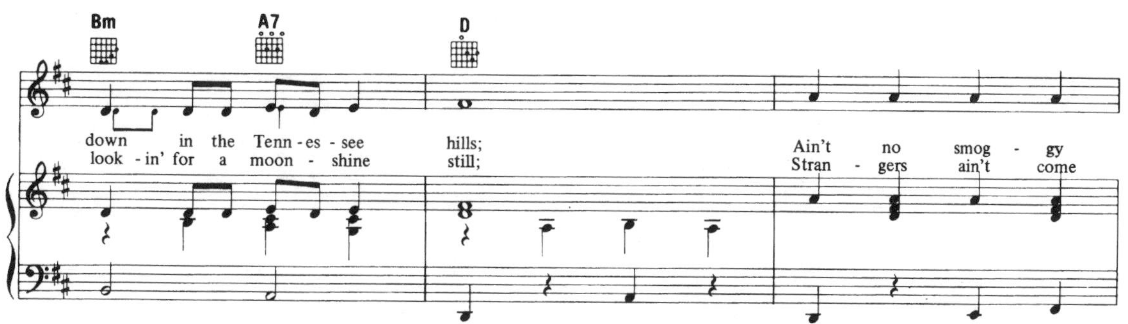

G D Bm A7

smoke on Rock - y Top; Ain't no tel - e - phone___
down from Rock - y Top; Reck - on they nev - er___

D G D

bills; Once I had a girl on Rock - y Top;
will; Corn won't grow at all on Rock - y Top;

Bm A7 D

Half bear, oth - er half cat; Wild as a mink, but
Dirt's too rock - y by far; That's why___ all the

G D Bm A7 D

sweet as sod - a pop, I still dream a - bout that;
folks on Rock - y Top get their corn___ from a - jar;

Verse 3:
I've had years of cramped-up city life
Trapped like a duck in a pen;
All I know is it's a pity life
Can't be simple again. (Chorus)

HL00304946

Texas

"Texas, Our Texas"

The state song of Texas is "Texas, Our Texas." The music was written by the late William J. Marsh (who died Feb. 1, 1971, in Fort Worth at age 90) and the words by Marsh and Gladys Yoakum Wright, both of Fort Worth. It was adopted as the result of an award offered by the Legislature. (Acts of 1929, first called session, Forty-first Legislature, p. 286.)

History source: *The 1986–87 Texas Almanac,* published by the A. H. Belo Corp.

Texas, Our Texas

a tempo
God bless you Tex - as! And keep you brave and strong, That
you may grow in power and worth, Thro' - out the ag - es long.
God bless you Tex-as! And keep you brave and strong, That you may grow in
power and worth Thro' - out the ag - es long.
last time
rall.
a tempo
rall. molto

Utah

"Utah, We Love Thee"

"Utah, We Love Thee" was written by Evan Stephens, who was born June 29, 1854, in Pencader, Carmarthenshire, South Wales, the tenth son of David and Jane Stephens. His parents joined the Church of Jesus Christ of Latter-day Saints (Mormon Church) and emigrated to Utah in 1866.

Stephens's formal education ended when his family left Wales; upon their arrival in Willard, Utah, Stephens worked as a farmhand until he was about 19 years old, when he got a job on the Utah Northern Railroad. Stephens was interested in music, but he was unable to afford a formal education, and so at age thirteen he started to borrow music books from the local choir in which he sang, in order to learn how to read music. He began composing music, eventually becoming a prolific composer of Latter-day Saint hymns. He moved to Logan, Utah, in 1880, and then to Salt Lake City in 1882 to teach music lessons. In 1885, he attended the New England Conservatory of Music for ten months, after which he returned to Salt Lake City and again taught singing lessons. Stephens was appointed director of the Mormon Tabernacle Choir in 1890. He increased the Choir's membership from 125 to more than 600, which facilitated the redesigning of the Choir section of the Salt Lake Tabernacle.

In mid-December of 1895, it looked as though Utah would finally obtain its long-sought dream of statehood, and committees were chosen for the "inaugural ceremonies." Evan Stephens was chosen to be the chairman of the music committee. For the ceremony he wrote "Utah, We Love Thee," and it was reported in *Salt Lake Tribune* (January 5, 1896) that "It is a rousing and bright chorus and many copies are being bought for souvenirs." It was performed by a chorus of 1,000 at the inaugural ceremonies on January 6 in the Salt Lake Tabernacle.

"Utah, We Love Thee" was first selected as the official state song in 1917 when Senate Joint Resolution 4 was signed by Governor Simon Bamberger on February 21. It was resubmitted in 1937 by Mrs. A. C. Lund, a member of the senate, from Salt Lake County and once more adopted on February 24, 1937, when Senate Bill 38 was signed by Governor Henry Hooper Blood (Utah Code 63-13-8).

History courtesy of Linda Thatcher, Librarian,
Utah State Historical Society,
Salt Lake City, Utah.

UTAH, WE LOVE THEE.

BY E. STEPHENS.

7520

NOTE.—This chorus may be sung as a male chorus, alone, or ladies chorus, alone, or a double, full, mixed chorus. If the latter, let each sing the lines and verses as indicated by the position of the words. Male lead 1st verse, ladies 2nd verse, alternate lines in 3rd, all joining the refrain "Utah we love thee" in each verse.

Vermont

"Hail, Vermont!"

The words and music for "Hail, Vermont!" were written by Josephine Hovey Perry.

Joint Resolution of the General Assembly (No. 350, *Laws of Vermont, 1937*) charged a committee to "select an official state song, which may be either a song in existence or one written for the purpose." "Hail, Vermont!" was chosen as the official state song from among 100 entries by this appointed committee of five persons.

"Hail, Vermont!" was selected as the official State Song of Vermont on May 12, 1938.

History compiled by Hladczuk and Hladczuk.

2
HAIL, VERMONT!
(Vermont's Official State Song)
Words and Music by
JOSEPHINE HOVEY PERRY
Allegretto con spirito
f
8
Ardently
f
Hail to Ver-mont! Love-ly Ver-mont! Hail to Ver-mont so fear - less!
Proud of Ver-mont, Love-ly Ver-mont, Proud of her charm and her beau - ty;
f
Sing we a song! Sing loud and long! To our lit - tle state so peer - less!
Proud of her name, Proud of her fame, We're proud of her sense of du - ty;
8
dolce
Green are her hills, Clear are her rills, Fair are her lakes and
Proud of her past, Proud first and last, Proud of her lands and
l.h.
dolce
3
3

riv - ers and val - leys; Blue are her skies,— Peace - ful she lies, But when
proud of her wa - ters; Her men are true blue, Her wo - men are— too, We're
l.h.
with spirit
roused to a call she speed - i - ly ral - lies!
proud of her sons and proud of her daugh-ters!
CHORUS
with fervor
Hail to Ver-mont!
Dear old Ver-mont! Our love for you is— great. We cher-ish your name, We
meno mosso
laud! We ACCLAIM! Our own Green Mountain State. We're
First ending
allargando
Second ending (Optional)
ritardando
Our own Green Mountain State.
allargando
ritardando

Virginia

"Carry Me Back to Old Virginia"

The music and lyrics to "Carry Me Back to Old Virginny" were written by James Allen Bland. Bland was a northern city-born and city-raised musician when he came to Virginia.

It has been reported that, on an antebellum trip to Tidewater, Virginia, Bland was so overwhelmingly impressed with the lay of the land, the bountifulness of the earth, and the sheer wonder of all that he heard and saw, that he seized upon a passing remark that a traveling companion had uttered, and fashioned it into a song.

That passing remark became the title to the State Song of Virginia, "Carry Me Back to Old Virginny."

James Bland was born in Flushing, New York in 1854. One of the first African-Americans to receive a college education, Bland was a successful minstrel performer as well as a lyricist and the composer of about 700 songs. "Carry Me Back to Old Virginny" written in 1878, is the most enduring and well-known of his songs. Bland also wrote "Golden Slippers" (1879), "In the Evening by the Moonlight" (1879), and "Hand Me Down My Walking Stick" (1880), to name but a few.

"Carry Me Back" was adopted as the official State Song of Virginia on February 22, 1940, as the result of House Joint Resolution No. 10. The version of the song as adopted used the word "Virginia" rather than "Virginny," as it was originally written.

History compiled by Hladczuk and Hladczuk.

CARRY ME BACK TO OLD VIRGINNY.

SONG AND CHORUS.

Words and Music by JAMES BLAND.

Author of "The Old Homestead," "In the morning by the bright light," &c., &c.

There's where the old dar - ke'ys heart am long'd to go, There's where I labored so
There's where this old dar - ke'ys life will pass a - way. Mas - sa and mis - sis have
hard for old mas - sa, Day af - ter day in the field of yel - low corn,
long gone before me, Soon we will meet on that bright and gold - en shore,
ritard.
No place on earth do I love more sin-cere -ly Than old Vir-gin - ny, the state where I was born.
There we'll be hap - py and free from all sorrow, There's where we'll meet and we'll nev - er part no more.
ritard.

CHORUS.
Soprano.
Car-ry me back to old Vir-gin-ny, There's where the cotton and the corn and tatoes grow,
Alto.
Tenor.
Car-ry me back to old Vir-gin-ny, There's where the cotton and the corn and tatoes grow,
Bass.
Piano.
f
ritard. Repeat pp last time.
There's where the birds warble sweet in the spring-time, There's where this old darkey's heart am long'd to go.
ritard.
There's where the birds warble sweet in the spring-time, There's where this old darkey's heart am long'd to go.
ritard.

Washington

"Washington My Home"

Helen Davis was born Helen Nancy Matson in Zanesville, Ohio, in November 1905. Her parents, Austin and Georgia Matson, were both descendants of pioneering Ohio families and had lived in Zanesville all their lives. Helen did not live in her hometown long enough to remember much about her family life, but she does remember that there was always music in her home. She says her parents had an abiding love for music and education and encouraged their children to excel in both.

Somewhere around 1908, Helen says her parents decided to pack up their household goods and move west to Denver, Colorado. Shortly after arriving they found a music teacher and started Helen out with lessons at the age of four. The lessons continued until she was eighteen.

When Helen was a teenager, her parents moved her and her brother Jim to the Okanogan county of Washington. As soon as she was old enough, she enrolled in college at Bellingham Normal School as a music major. Although she did not graduate from college, due to a shortage of funds, she did complete more than a year and a half of her studies.

Helen met and eventually married Chauncey Davis, a native of Mt. Vernon, Washington, while attending college. In the late 1920s, Chauncey accepted a job in Pacific County as superintendent of the grade school in the town of Long Beach.

Throughout these years, Helen says she was busy raising a family and being a housewife. However, she did not neglect her music. Whenever possible she performed solo for civic groups or helped her husband organize school musical performances. She also played the piano at the local Methodist churches.

On November 6, 1934, Helen's husband Chauncey was elected County Superintendent of Schools. Since the job required Chauncey's presence at the courthouse, the family moved fifty miles north to South Bend. It was the last move Helen ever had to make.

The move to South Bend did not change Helen's life much in the early years. Helen's life did change, however, in the 1940s when a local outbreak of tuberculosis got her involved in the national campaign to eradicate it.

Eventually, as Helen's involvement in the TB campaign decreased, her interests in other community projects increased. Two endeavors that gave her immense satisfaction were her contributions to the South Bend Beautification Committee and her work with teenagers.

Helen is proud of all the teenagers she worked with in the 1940s and '50s, and still recalls all of their names, but one group of six South Bend girls still remains her favorite. She named the group the "Logger's Daughters" and traveled with them throughout the county and state, performing musical numbers that she wrote and staged.

Staging and composing songs for Logger's Daughters performances was pleasant work for Helen and made her eager for similar musical projects. The appropriate challenge came her way in 1949 when she was enlisted to write the music for an operetta about the early years of Washington's logging industry. Several rewrites later the operetta became a musical called *Eliza and the Lumberjack.*

Eliza is not the only musical production Helen has written and composed. She has also produced a pageant celebrating Pacific County's first 110 years as a county.

While preparing the Pacific County Centennial, Helen searched for a song to be the show's centerpiece. She says she wanted one that would stir the crowd with pride and be remembered beyond the celebration. Someone suggested "Washington Beloved" (a 1909 anthem written by Edmond S. Meany and Reginald De Koven), but Helen decided it wasn't what she wanted. Eventually she chose a song she had composed years earlier called "America, My Home." The combination of music and lyrics brought tears to many eyes and was hailed in newspaper reviews from Seattle to Portland.

Shortly after the centennial programs of 1951, Helen decided to change the title of her composition to "Washington My Home." The simple change of title made the song more appealing, and it wasn't long before civic clubs were opening their meetings with it. In 1956, the Washington State Federation of Music Clubs adopted it as its official song and promoted it around the state. Popular acceptance of the song as the state anthem ultimately led state politicians to make it the official state song in March 1959.

History by Larry J. Weathers. First produced in the *Sou'wester,* Vol. 19 (Winter 1984).

WASHINGTON MY HOME

arranged by Stuart Churchill

Helen Davis

REFRAIN
Am B♭ Am C7 Fsus. F Am6 Gm7 C7 Gm7 C7
Wash-ing-ton my home; Where ev-er I may roam; This is my land, my
Gm7 C7 Gm7 C7 C+ F F F♯dim.
na-tive land, Wash-ing-ton, my home. Our ver-dant for-est green, Ca-
Gm7 C7 Gm7 C7 Gm7 C7 Gm7 C6
ressed by sil - v'ry stream. From moun-tain peak To fields of wheat, Wash-ing-ton, my
Fsus. F B♭ F Gm7 C6 C9 F
home. There's peace you feel and un-der-stand In this, our own be-lov-ed land. We

Bb F Em Dm7 G7 C Dm7 C7 F Fmaj.7
greet the day with head held high, And for-ward ev-er is our cry. We'll hap-py ev-er
p
F C7 Gm7 C7 Gm7 C7
be As peo-ple al-ways free. For you and me a des-tin-y;
f
mf
1st Gm7 C6 C7 Fsus. F C9 C6
Wash-ing-ton my home.
2nd. Gm7 Am C#dim. Dm sus. Dm F7
Wash-ing-ton, my home. For
Bb F7 Bb G7b5 F F+ Dm Gm b5 C7sus. C7 F
you and me a des-tin-y; Wash-ing-ton, my home.

West Virginia

"West Virginia, My Sweet Home"

"West Virginia, My Sweet Home" was written by Col. Julian G. Hearne of Wheeling, West Virginia.

Col. Hearne was born in Wheeling, West Virginia, in September of 1904. He attended the Linsly Institute, the Manlius School, Washington and Jefferson College, and West Virginia University Law School, where he received his law degree in 1930.

In the fall of 1945, Col. Hearne had just returned home from military duty in the Pacific. In the spring of 1946, Col. Hearne was inspired by the natural beauty of West Virginia. Knowing that the state did not have a state song, Col. Hearne decided that he would write the music and lyrics for one.

"West Virginia, My Sweet Home" was proclaimed by the state legislature in 1947 as the official song of the state of West Virginia.

The copyright ownership for the song "West Virginia, My Sweet Home" could not be ascertained.

History compiled by Hladczuk and Hladczuk.

"The West Virginia Hills"

In 1961, the 55th Legislature of West Virginia designated the composition known as "The West Virginia Hills," words by Mrs. Ellen King and music by H. E. Engle, to be "the" official state song. However, in 1947 the 48th Legislature had designated "West Virginia, My Home Sweet Home" as "one" of the official state songs. Therefore, in 1963, both songs were redesignated as official state songs along with "This Is My West Virginia," which was designated as the official centennial song.

Ellen Amanda Ruddell was born on April 22, 1846, in Glenville, West Virginia. She married the Reverend David H. King, who was then pastor of the Presbyterian church in Punxsutawney, Pennsylvania. From 1880 to 1887, the Kings lived in Lonaconing, Maryland. Reverend King then became pastor of the Presbyterian church in Wildwood, New Jersey, where he was pastor for 25 of the 35 years they resided there. In May of 1921, Mrs. King moved with her husband to Hollywood, California, and lived there until her death in the summer of 1927.

Mrs. Ellen King is regarded as the author of the words to the popular state song, but some accounts claim her husband as actually writing the poem and having it published in her name in the *Glenville Crescent* during a visit to her family home.

Henry Everett Engle is credited with reading the poem in that newspaper and being so inspired as to write the music. The date of this has been given as 1879, 1883, and 1885 in various sources, but the Barbour County Historical Society gives 1879 as the date.

Mr. H. E. Engle was born on September 30, 1849, in Barbour County, about three miles from Philippi. His father was William and his mother was the former Tabitha Criss. By the time he was 16 he was composing songs, and around the age of 21 he studied music for several months at Singers Glen, Virginia. By the time he was 23, he had published a small booklet called *Beautiful Songs.* His family moved to Tanner in Gilmer County, where he continued to write music as well as teach school and singing classes. In 1885 he married Julia Lloyd of Lloydsville in Braxton County. They had a son, Aldine.

Henry Everett Engle published a collection of songs titled *The West Virginia Singer* as well as many other songs, but his best known composition was the music to "The West Virginia Hills." Most of his songs were religious in nature and, being an ardent prohibitionist, he wrote at least two songs for the cause of temperance.

He devoted much of his life to farming and he died on his farm on April 12, 1933.

History compiled by Hladczuk and Hladczuk.

"This Is My West Virginia"

"This Is My West Virginia" was written by Ms. Iris Bell of Charleston, West Virginia. The song is not only one of the official songs of West Virginia but it has also been designated as the official centennial song.

It has been reported that Ms. Bell was inspired by two fellow West Virginians: her grandfather, John E. Good of Sissonville, West Virginia, and Colonel A. E. Humphreys, Good's brother-in-law.

At the time that the song was written, Ms. Bell was the only female band leader in the Charleston, West Virginia, area. She wrote the words and music to "This Is My West Virginia" in about 30 minutes, in the middle of the night.

"This Is My West Virginia" was adopted as an official song of West Virginia, by House Concurrent Resolution No. 19, on February 28, 1963.

Permission to use "This Is My West Virginia" could not be obtained.

History compiled by Hladczuk and Hladczuk.

West Virginia Hills 5

Mrs. ELLEN KING

H. E. ENGLE

Wisconsin

"On, Wisconsin!"

The music for "On, Wisconsin!" was composed in 1909 by William T. Purdy with the idea of entering it in a Minnesota contest for the creation of a new football song. Instead, a friend, Carl Beck, persuaded Purdy to dedicate the song to the University of Wisconsin football team and collaborated in the effort by writing the lyrics. The song was introduced at the University of Wisconsin in November 1909. It was later acclaimed by John Philip Sousa as the best college song he ever heard.

Lyrics more in keeping with the purposes of a state song were subsequently written in 1913 by J. S. Hubbard (then editor of the *Beloit Free Press*) and Judge (later Tax Commissioner) Charles D. Rosa. Hubbard and Rosa were among the delegates from many states convened in 1913 to commemorate the centennial of the Battle of Lake Erie, where Oliver Hazard Perry defeated the British fleet near Put-in-Bay, Ohio. Inspired by the occasion, they provided new, more solemn words to the already well-known Wisconsin football song. Some of their lyrics were later incorporated in the official state song.

Although "On, Wisconsin!" was recognized everywhere as Wisconsin's song, the state did not officially adopt it until 1959. In that year, Assemblyman Harold W. Clemens discovered that his state was one of only ten states without a song and introduced a bill to give "On, Wisconsin!" the status he thought it deserved. Indeed, as a vocalist, he had sung "On, Wisconsin!" at public gatherings for many years thinking it was the state song. On discovering that many different lyrics existed, an official text for the first verse of what was to become the state anthem was incorporated in the bill. It was enacted as Chapter 170, Laws of 1959, amending statute Section 1.10.

History source: *Wisconsin Blue Book,* 1987–1988.

On, Wisconsin!

March-Song and Two-Step.

Words by CARL BECK. Music by W. T. PURDY.

* Run the ball 'round Minnesota.
On, Wisconsin! 3—2.

On, Wisconsin! 3—3.

Wyoming

"Wyoming March Song"

According to Charles E. Winter, the song as written by himself and Mr. Clemens proved a great success, but it did not lend itself readily to popular singing because of its extreme vocal range.

In the early part of the year 1920, Professor George E. Knapp, Professor of Voice at the State University at Laramie, composed new music in march time and a more singable range. This immediately proved itself adapted to popular singing. The fact that the new music lent itself to the march and dance secured for it general acceptance.

On February 15, 1955, the song was adopted as the state song.

History courtesy of the Wyoming State Archives, Museums and Historical Department, Historical Research and Publications Division.

3

WYOMING
March Song

4
A little slower
breast of this great land; Where the mas - sive Rock-ies stand, There's Wy -
rose and red it springs, White the but - ton and its rings, Thou art
gran - it bas - es deep, 'Neath thy bos - om's broad-ened sweep, Lie the
chil - dren thou dost teach, Na - ture's truth thou givst to each, Free and
is, Wy - o - ming's star, Home it leads me near or far; O Wy -
o - ming young and strong, the State I love!
loy - al for they're red and white and blue.
rich - es that have gained and brought thee fame.
no - ble are thy work - ings and thy ways.
o - ming all my heart and love you've won!
REFRAIN
a tempo
Wy - o - ming! Wy - o - ming! Land of the sun - light clear, Wy -
Wyoming March Song - 3 & Quar.

5
o - ming! Wy - o - ming! Land that we hold so dear. Wy-
o - ming! Wy - o - ming! Prec - ious art thou and thine; Wy-
o - ming! Wy - o - ming! Be - lov - ed state of mine!
Wyoming March Song - 3 & Quar.

Index of Song Titles

About the Authors

John Hladczuk (B.S., M.S., The University of Tennessee-Knoxville; Ph.D., The State University of New York at Buffalo) has published and worked in the areas of literacy, reading, sports law, and music. His prior books include *Comparative Reading, Literacy/Illiteracy in the World, General Issues in Literacy/Illiteracy, Sports Law and Legislation,* and the classic *International Handbook of Reading Education.* He is currently co-director of the *State Song Project.*

Sharon Schneider Hladczuk (B.S., M.S., Ph.D., The State University of New York at Buffalo) is currently pursuing interests in the arts, spirituality, and women's issues. Her prior publications include *Literacy/Illiteracy in the World, General Issues in Literacy/Illiteracy, and Sports Law and Legislation.*